AAT

Management Accounting: Budgeting

Level 4

Course Book

For assessments from
1 September 2016

First edition June 2016

ISBN 9781 4727 4818 8
ISBN (for internal use only) 9781 4727 4874 4

British Library Cataloguing-in-Publication Data
A catalogue record for this book is available from the British Library

Published by

BPP Learning Media Ltd
BPP House, Aldine Place
142-144 Uxbridge Road
London W12 8AA

www.bpp.com/learningmedia

Printed in the United Kingdom by Wheatons Exeter Ltd
Hennock Road
Marsh Barton
Exeter
EX2 8RP

Contents

Introduction to the course

Syllabus overview

This unit is about forecasting and preparing budgets. The learner will develop the necessary skills and knowledge to allow them to prepare a range of budgets, analyse variances and make recommendations for improving organisational performance. They will be able to inform managers of financial forecasts to aid organisational planning and control.

Test specification for this unit assessment

Assessment method	Marking type	Duration of assessment
Computer based assessment	Partially computer/ partially human marked	2.5 hours

Learning outcomes		Weighting
1	Prepare forecasts of income and expenditure	10%
2	Prepare budgets	35%
3	Demonstrate how budgeting can improve organisational performance	35%
4	Report budgetary information to management in a clear and appropriate format	20%
Total		**100%**

Assessment structure

2½ hours duration

Competency is 70%

*Note that this is only a guideline as to what might come up. The format and content of each task may vary from what we have listed below.

Your assessment will consist of 8 tasks

Task	Max marks	Expected Content*	Chapter Ref	Study complete
1	20	**Organisation and coding** A number of small exercises: Examples of areas that might be tested (this list is not exhaustive): • Selecting appropriate sources of information for various data sources eg pay rates from HR department • Identifying which managers need to participate in various aspects of budget preparation & explanation of variances • Select the appropriate sections of the budget for cost headings • Selecting appropriate accounting treatment of cost items such as raw materials (direct cost) • Forecasting data	Cost classification and behaviour/ Forecasting data/ Budgetary Control Systems	
2	20	**Production resources** Exercises covering aspects of 'physical' planning & scheduling. Examples of areas that might be tested (this list is not exhaustive): • Production plan • Calculation of process losses • Plans of material • Plans of labour • Plans of plant/equipment • Calculation of capacity constraints	Budget preparation /Budgetary control – limiting factors	

BPP LEARNING MEDIA

Task	Max marks	Expected Content*	Chapter Ref	Study complete
3	20	**Operating Budget, Cash flow** Examples of areas that might be tested (this list is not exhaustive): • Completion of working schedules and an operating budget in a conventional manufacturing account format. All of the required data including a simple production plan is provided. • Cash flow forecast	Budget preparation /Preparing cash budgets	
4	20	**Present a budget for approval** The scope of this task is quite broad. A report, in the form of an email in a number of parts is required: Examples of areas that might be tested (this list is not exhaustive): • Explain the sources of relevant data used in budget proposals • Explain key planning assumptions made • Explain which assumptions are within the control of management • Recommend performance measures A question might require a candidate to use the facts given in the question for the first part, and then draw on their knowledge and make recommendations, for the next part(s).	Forecasting/ Budgetary Control/ Performance Indicators in Budgetary Control	
5	20	**Breaking budgets into accounting periods/Revising budgets** Examples of areas that might be tested (this list is not exhaustive): • Breaking the annual budget into accounting periods. This is a test of logic & calculation, the breakdown must be consistent with the way actual results will be reported or the variances will be meaningless. • Revising an operating budget to illustrate the impact of changing assumptions, eg consumption of resources decreasing rather than increasing.	Forecasting/ Budget Preparation/	

vi

BPP
LEARNING MEDIA

Task	Max marks	Expected Content*	Chapter Ref	Study complete
6	20	**Standard costing and budget flexing** Examples of areas that might be tested (this list is not exhaustive): • Exercises involving flexing budgets and comparing actual results to the flexed budget	Budget preparation /Budgetary control – comparing budget and actual costs	
7	20	**Operating statement** Completion of an operating statement, where the 'original' budget is provided but it must then be flexed and variances entered. You might also be required to calculate the variances. Notes will explain the behaviour of costs, including variable, semi-variable, stepped and fixed.	Budget preparation /Budgetary control – comparing budget and actual costs	
8	20	**Performance report** Examples of areas that might be tested (this list is not exhaustive): • Identify significant variances • Use the operational information provided to explaining the likely cause of variances • Identify and describe important budgetary planning and control issues • Make relevant and focused recommendations to initiate management action • Explain the behavioural aspects of budgeting	Budgetary Control Systems – Budgetary Control – comparing budget and actual costs/ Performance Indicators in Budgetary Control	

Skills bank

Our experience of preparing students for this type of assessment suggests that to obtain competency, you will need to develop a number of key skills.

What do I need to know to do well in the assessment?

Budgeting is examined by numeric entry, use of picklists, and written tasks. This means that you need a broad and yet quite detailed knowledge of the syllabus as well as an understanding of the concepts and techniques involved.

The type of knowledge that you have to acquire includes the following:

Theoretical knowledge – the fundamental definitions and basic thinking behind different management accounting techniques. These will often be tested in narrative questions.

Practical knowledge – the application of techniques to 'real life' situations. These will often be tested in numerical questions, but you will also have to demonstrate your understanding of key data (such as variances and performance indicators) via a discussion of what these mean for a company.

In this section we will look at approaches that you can take to help you learn the key elements of the knowledge in the syllabus, and develop your application skills.

Learning the theory

In the exam you will encounter questions that test your knowledge of key management accounting theory.

You should therefore make sure you learn the most important bits of detail for each topic or technique. This should include formulae for numerical techniques. You may like to use the overview diagrams in the notes as a base.

Doing this will set you on your way to achieving the breadth of knowledge you need across the syllabus. It will also give you an excellent foundation on which to begin to apply your knowledge to the wide range of questions you'll see in the exam.

Application

Being able to apply your fundamental syllabus knowledge to the situations presented in exam questions is of vital importance.

During your studies, you must gradually build up your exposure to exam style questions so that you can become 'flexible' and able to deal with whatever questions you see in your exam.

Don't be discouraged if you struggle with application questions on a particular topic – just take this as an indication that there are still a few gaps in your knowledge of the theory. You can then pinpoint exactly where you need to review your notes before continuing with more question practice. This really is an excellent way to prepare for the exam.

Assumed knowledge

Management Accounting: Budgeting is a **mandatory** unit. Its content links with *Management Accounting: Decision and Control* but the application here is specifically to budgeting.

Assessment style

In the assessment you will complete tasks by:

1 Entering narrative by selecting from drop down menus of narrative options known as **picklists**

2 Using **drag and drop** menus to enter narrative

3 Typing in numbers, known as **gapfill** entry

4 Entering **ticks**

5 Free **text boxes** for answering written tasks

You must familiarise yourself with the style of the online questions and the AAT software before taking the assessment. As part of your revision, login to the **AAT website** and attempt their **online practice assessments**.

Introduction to the assessment

The question practice you do will prepare you for the format of tasks you will see in the *Management Accounting: Budgeting* assessment. It is also useful to familiarise yourself with the introductory information you **may** be given at the start of the assessment. For example:

You have 2 hours and 30 minutes to this sample assessment.

This assessment contains 8 tasks and you should attempt to complete every task.

Each task is independent. You will not need to refer to your answers to previous tasks.

Read every task carefully to make sure you understand what is required.

Where the date is relevant, it is given in the task data.

Both minus signs and brackets can be used to indicate negative numbers unless task instructions say otherwise.

You must use a full stop to indicate a decimal point. For example, write 100.57 NOT 100,57 OR 100 57.

You may use a comma to indicate a number in the thousands, but you don't have to. For example, 10000 and 10,000 are both OK.

1   As you revise, use the **BPP Passcards** to consolidate your knowledge. They are a pocket-sized revision tool, perfect for packing in that last-minute revision.

2   Attempt as many tasks as possible in the **Question Bank**. There are plenty of assessment-style tasks which are excellent preparation for the real assessment.

3   Always **check** through your own answers as you will in the real assessment, before looking at the solutions in the back of the Question Bank.

Key to icons

	Key term	A key definition which is important to be aware of for the assessment
	Formula to learn	A formula you will need to learn as it will not be provided in the assessment
	Formula provided	A formula which is provided within the assessment and generally available as a pop-up on screen
	Activity	An example which allows you to apply your knowledge to the technique covered in the Course Book. The solution is provided at the end of the chapter
	Illustration	A worked example which can be used to review and see how an assessment question could be answered
	Assessment focus point	A high priority point for the assessment
	Open book reference	Where use of an open book will be allowed for the assessment
	Real life examples	A practical real life scenario

AAT qualifications

The material in this book may support the following AAT qualifications:

AAT Professional Diploma in Accounting Level 4, AAT Professional Diploma in Accounting at SCQF Level 8 and Certificate: Accounting (Level 5 AATSA).

Supplements

From time to time we may need to publish supplementary materials to one of our titles. This can be for a variety of reasons, from a small change in the AAT unit guidance to new legislation coming into effect between editions.

You should check our supplements page regularly for anything that may affect your learning materials. All supplements are available free of charge on our supplements page on our website at:

www.bpp.com/learning-media/about/students

Improving material and removing errors

There is a constant need to update and enhance our study materials in line with both regulatory changes and new insights into the assessments.

From our team of authors BPP appoints a subject expert to update and improve these materials for each new edition.

Their updated draft is subsequently technically checked by another author and from time to time non-technically checked by a proof reader.

We are very keen to remove as many numerical errors and narrative typos as we can but given the volume of detailed information being changed in a short space of time we know that a few errors will sometimes get through our net.

We apologise in advance for any inconvenience that an error might cause. We continue to look for new ways to improve these study materials and would welcome your suggestions. Please feel free to contact our AAI Head of Programme at nisarahmed@bpp.com if you have any suggestions for us.

Cost classification and behaviour

1

Learning outcomes

2.1	**Identify budgetary responsibilities and accountabilities**
	• Classify and allocate direct costs to appropriate responsibility centres
	• Identify appropriate responsibility centres and recovery methods for all types of indirect cost
2.4	**Calculate budgets for different types of cost**
	• Direct
	• Indirect
	• Fixed
	• Variable
	• Semi-variable
	• Stepped
	• Capital
	• Revenue

Assessment context

Cost classification and behaviour is essential knowledge used in many of the management accounting techniques.

Qualification context

Cost classification and behaviour is tested in *Management Accounting: Budgeting* and *Management Accounting: Decision and Control* at Level 4.

Business context

Grouping costs together is essential for a business to be able to analyse costs, budget and plan effectively.

Chapter overview

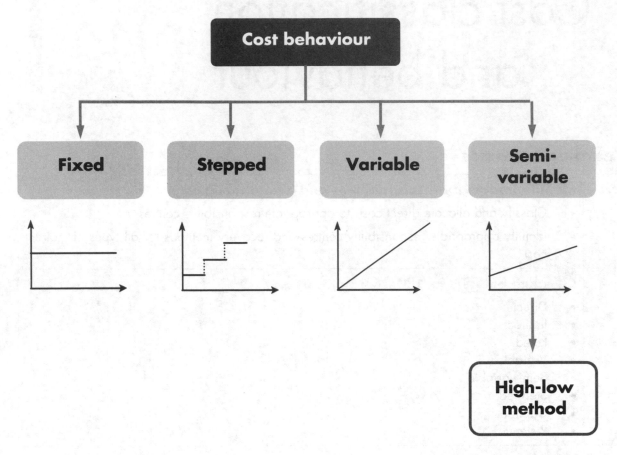

Cost behaviour

- Fixed
- Stepped
- Variable
- Semi-variable

High-low method

- Used to split fixed and variable elements
- Find highest and lowest activity levels and their associated costs
- Subtract low from high
- Use remainder to calculate variable cost per unit
- Substitute variable cost per unit back into high or low total cost formula to calculate the fixed cost

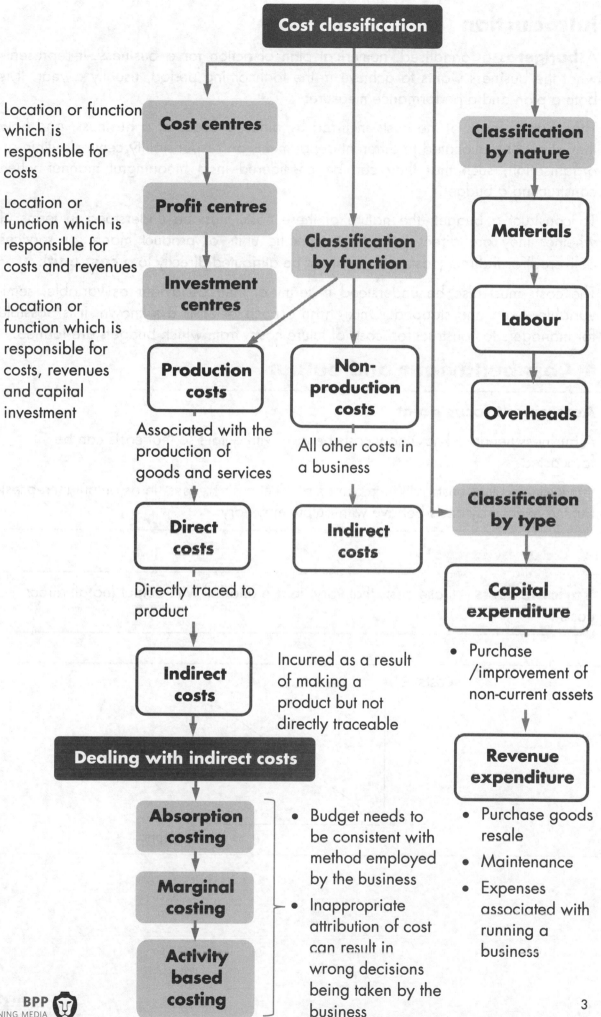

Location or function which is responsible for costs

Location or function which is responsible for costs and revenues

Location or function which is responsible for costs, revenues and capital investment

Cost classification

Cost centres

Profit centres

Investment centres

Classification by function

Production costs

Associated with the production of goods and services

Direct costs

Directly traced to product

Indirect costs

Dealing with indirect costs

Absorption costing

Marginal costing

Activity based costing

Non-production costs

All other costs in a business

Indirect costs

Incurred as a result of making a product but not directly traceable

- Budget needs to be consistent with method employed by the business
- Inappropriate attribution of cost can result in wrong decisions being taken by the business

Classification by nature

Materials

Labour

Overheads

Classification by type

Capital expenditure

- Purchase /improvement of non-current assets

Revenue expenditure

- Purchase goods resale
- Maintenance
- Expenses associated with running a business

Introduction

A **budget** is a formalised, numerical plan of action for a business. It represents what the business wants to achieve in the forthcoming period, usually a year. It is both a plan and a performance measure.

This chapter looks at the costs incurred by different areas of a business, and how they should be allocated to different departments or 'responsibility centres' within an organisation, such that they can be considered in a meaningful manner when constructing a budget.

To construct a budget, the nature of these costs must be understood in terms of whether they are direct (relating to specific units of product made, or services delivered) or indirect (costs which cannot be attributed directly to a **cost unit**).

The costs must also be understood in terms of their behaviour as variable, semi-variable, fixed and stepped. Once these aspects of costs are known, it is possible for managers to construct forecasts of future costs, from which budgets are formed.

1 Cost behaviour and output

Assessment focus point

A business needs to know how costs behave with output so that costs can be forecasted.

It is expected that costs will increase as production increases (ie as output increases) but the exact way costs behave with output may vary.

1.1 Variable costs

Key term

Variable costs – those costs that vary, ie rise and fall with output (eg all direct costs).

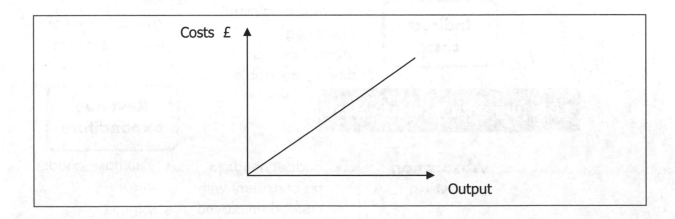

1.2 Fixed costs

Key term

Fixed costs – those costs that will not vary with output, ie fixed overheads (eg rent and rates).

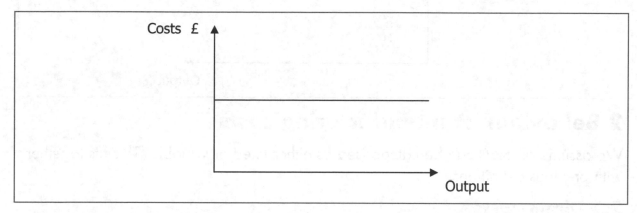

1.3 Stepped fixed costs

Key term

Stepped fixed costs – a fixed cost within certain levels of activity. These costs remain fixed for a certain level of output and then increase until a further level of output is reached (eg supervisors' costs, rent).

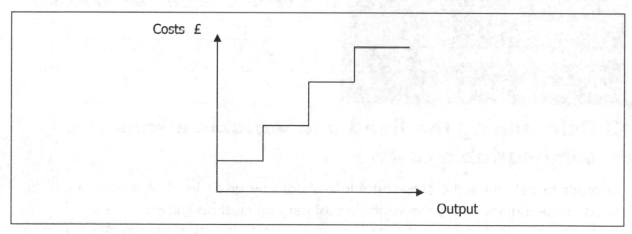

1.4 Semi-variable (Mixed) costs

Key term

Semi-variable (Mixed) costs – those costs which are part fixed and part variable, and are therefore partly affected by changes in the level of activity (eg telephone).

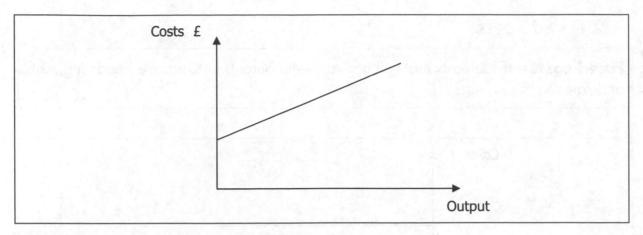

2 Behaviour of manufacturing costs

We assume all costs can be categorised as either fixed or variable. This fits together with previous definitions.

2.1 Direct costs

By their nature, **direct costs** will be variable costs.

2.2 Indirect costs/overheads

Overheads can be fixed (eg rent) or variable (eg tool hire).

	Fixed	Variable
Direct costs	X	✓
Production overheads	✓	✓
Non-manufacturing costs	✓	✓

3 Determining the fixed and variable elements of semi-variable costs

In order to determine the semi-variable costs at any given level of activity, both the fixed element amount and the variable cost per unit must be known.

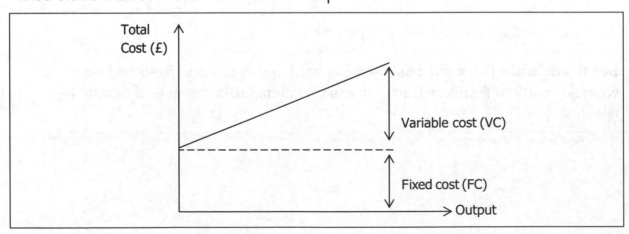

The total of a **semi-variable cost** can be expressed as:

Formula to learn

Total cost = Fixed element + (Variable cost per unit x Number of units)

Illustration 1: Classification of costs by behaviour

Here is a comprehensive example of the use of all the cost behaviour principles described above to forecast production costs.

Cameron Ltd will produce one product, which requires the following inputs, in the forthcoming quarter:

Direct materials	1 kg @ £3.50 per kg
Direct labour	1 hour @ £6.00 per hour
Rent	£4,000 per quarter
Leased machines	£1,500 for every 4,000 units of production
Maintenance costs	£1,000 per quarter plus £1.00 per unit

Calculate the budgeted total cost of production and the budgeted cost per unit for each of the following production levels for the coming quarter:

(a)   **4,000 units**
(b)   **10,000 units**
(c)   **16,000 units**

Direct materials – this is a **variable cost** with a constant amount per unit (1 kg × £3.50 = £3.50). Therefore, the total cost is found by multiplying the number of units by the unit cost:

£3.50 × 4,000 units	=	£14,000
£3.50 × 10,000 units	=	£35,000
£3.50 × 16,000 units	=	£56,000

Direct labour – another **variable cost**, with a unit cost of 1 hr × £6 = £6:

£6.00 × 4,000 units	=	£24,000
£6.00 × 10,000 units	=	£60,000
£6.00 × 16,000 units	=	£96,000

Rent – this is a **fixed cost** and therefore, provided we are still operating within the **relevant range**, it will remain at £4,000, whatever the production level.

Leased machines – this is a **stepped cost** and the number of machines leased will depend upon the quantity of production:

4,000 units	=	1 machine	=	£1,500
10,000 units	=	3 machines	=	£4,500
16,000 units	=	4 machines	=	£6,000

Maintenance costs – this is a **semi-variable cost** with a fixed element of £1,000 and a variable cost of £1 per unit. The total cost for each activity level is:

4,000 units	=	£1,000 + (4,000 × £1.00)	=	£5,000
10,000 units	=	£1,000 + (10,000 × £1.00)	=	£11,000
16,000 units	=	£1,000 + (16,000 × £1.00)	=	£17,000

Thus, the total costs of production are:

	Production level – units		
	4,000	10,000	16,000
	£	£	£
Direct materials (variable)	14,000	35,000	56,000
Direct labour (variable)	24,000	60,000	96,000
Rent (fixed)	4,000	4,000	4,000
Leased machines (stepped)	1,500	4,500	6,000
Maintenance costs	5,000	11,000	17,000
Total cost	48,500	114,500	179,000
Number of units	4,000	10,000	16,000
Cost per unit	£12.13	£11.45	£11.19

The cost per unit will decrease if the production quantity increases. This is because the fixed cost and the fixed element of the semi-variable cost will then be spread over a larger number of units.

Variable costs with a discount

Suppose now that the supplier of the materials offers a bulk purchasing discount of 6% for all purchases if an order is placed for more than 8,000 kg.

What is the direct materials cost in total, and per unit, at each level of production?

4,000 units

Total cost	4,000 × £3.50	=	£14,000
Cost per unit	£14,000/4,000	=	£3.50

10,000 units

Total cost	10,000 × (£3.50 × 94%)	=	£32,900
Cost per unit	£32,900/10,000	=	£3.29

16,000 units

Total cost	16,000 × (£3.50 × 94%)	=	£52,640
Cost per unit	£52,640/16,000	=	£3.29

The direct materials are now not a true variable cost, as the cost per unit falls once production is in excess of 8,000 units.

3.1 High-low method for semi-variable costs

Assessment focus point

This is a four-step method.

1. Select the highest and lowest activity level and their costs
2. Find the difference in the output and costs
3. Calculate the variable cost per unit
4. Calculate the fixed cost

Activity 1: High-low calculation

The total costs of a business for differing levels of output are as follows.

Output (units)	Total Costs
10,000	27,000
12,000	31,000
14,000	35,000

Required

Calculate the variable cost/unit and the fixed cost.

	Output	Cost
Highest		
Lowest		
	_____	_____

Total costs
Variable cost
∴ Fixed cost
_____

Illustration 2: High-Low method

The following data has been collected from a business:

Units produced	5,000	7,500	10,000
Total costs (£)	54,500	76,500	90,000

Total costs are made up of two elements, a fixed cost (that changes when the units exceed 7,000) and some variable costs, which remain constant per unit.

Here we calculate the total fixed costs at production levels below and above 7,000 units and the variable cost per unit.

High-low method above volume of 7,000 units.

	Output	Cost
Highest	10,000	90,000
Lowest	7,500	76,500
	2,500	13,500

∴ VC/unit =   £13,500/2,500 = £5.40

NB. This is constant at all volumes of output

TC = FC + VC/unit × output

Substitute at lowest (or highest) level:

£76,500 = FC + £5.40 × 7,500

FC = £36,000 above output of 7,000 units.

So at 5,000 units:

TC = FC + VC/unit x output

£54,500 = FC + £5.40 × 5,000

FC = £27,500 below output of 7,000 units.

Remember, not all costs follow the textbook profiles. For example, direct labour is often described as a variable cost. In reality, basic wages are often fixed and overtime is then paid at a higher rate, should it be required.

4 Cost classification

Cost classification is the arrangement of cost items into logical groups, for example, by their **type** (capital and revenue expenditure), their **function** (administration, production etc) or by their **nature** (materials, wages etc).

The eventual aim of costing is to determine the cost of producing a product/service.

4.1 Capital expenditure vs revenue expenditure

Capital expenditure includes:

- The purchase of non-current assets
- The improvement of the earning capability of non-current assets

Revenue expenditure includes:

- The purchase of goods for resale
- The maintenance of the existing earning capacity of non-current assets
- Expenditure incurred in conducting the business

Capital expenditure is shown as a non-current asset in the statement of financial position, while revenue expenditure is charged as a cost in the income statement.

4.2 Direct and indirect costs

Production costs can be split into direct costs and indirect costs.

4.2.1 Direct costs

Direct costs are those costs which can be **specifically identified** with, and allocated to, a single cost unit.

Key term

Prime costs – total direct costs.

4.2.2 Indirect production costs

Key term

Indirect production costs – those costs which are incurred in the course of making a product/service but which **cannot be identified with a particular cost unit**.

Indirect production costs are often referred to as production **overheads**.

Illustration 3: Identifying direct and indirect costs

Here are some of the costs involved in making chocolate bars, grouped by direct and indirect costs.

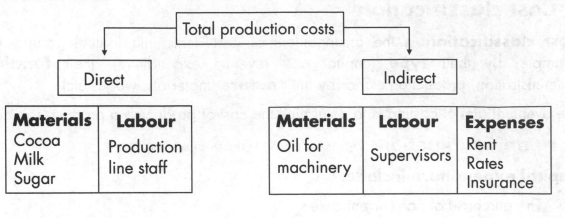

Total production costs

Direct

Materials	**Labour**
Cocoa	Production
Milk	line staff
Sugar	

Indirect

Materials	**Labour**	**Expenses**
Oil for	Supervisors	Rent
machinery		Rates
		Insurance

4.3 Classification by function

A company may first arrange cost items into groups by function. At the highest level, there could be groups of production costs and groups of non-production costs.

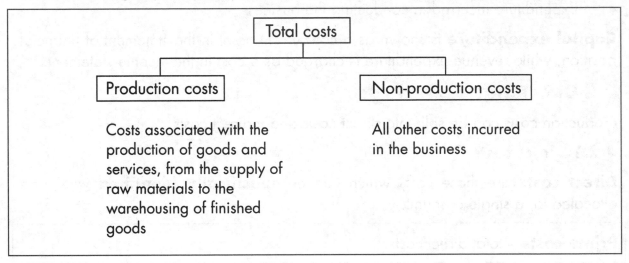

Total costs

Production costs

Costs associated with the production of goods and services, from the supply of raw materials to the warehousing of finished goods

Non-production costs

All other costs incurred in the business

4.4 Classification by nature

Production costs can then be broken down further **by their nature**.

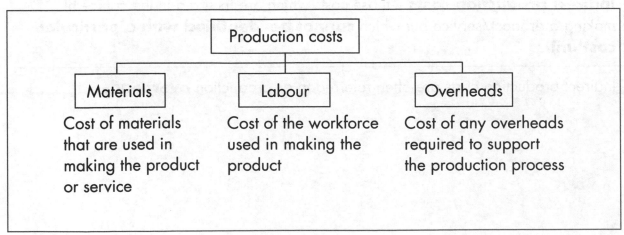

Production costs

Materials

Cost of materials that are used in making the product or service

Labour

Cost of the workforce used in making the product

Overheads

Cost of any overheads required to support the production process

Non-production costs can also be broken down further by their nature to aid analysis.

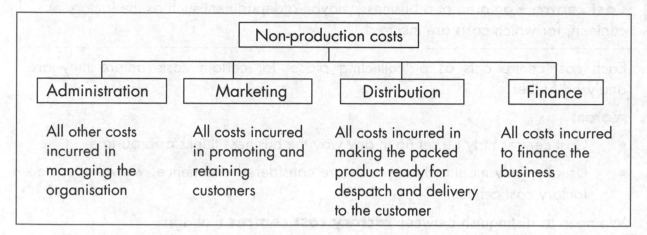

Illustration 4: Classifying costs

The following items of expenditure can be classified by the headings below.

Administration	Marketing and distribution	Capital Expenditure	Cash flow
Depreciation charge of office equipment	Sales staff salaries	Factory extension	Payments to suppliers
Finance director's salary	Advertising	Van purchase	
Accounts staff salaries	Drivers' salaries		
Office staff salaries	Packing materials		
	Lorry repairs		

5 Responsibility centres

To structure an overall budget, the various department and functions within an organisation can be classified in terms of their purpose and responsibilities, into responsibility centres. These can be cost centres, profit centres or investment centres.

This means that each centre has responsibility for the costs or revenues in its budget, and actual results will then be compared to budgets for each centre, to monitor and control performance.

5.1 Cost centres

Cost centre – an area of a business, maybe a department such as the factory or canteen, for which costs are incurred.

Each cost centre acts as a 'collecting place' for certain costs before they are analysed further.

Notes:

- Cost centres may be set up in any way the business thinks appropriate.

- Usually, only manufacturing costs are considered and hence, we will focus on factory cost centres.

We need to distinguish between **factory cost centres** that are:

- **Production cost centres**, directly involved in the production or provision of the cost unit, such as the assembly department

- **Service cost centres**, which support/service the production cost centres, eg the canteen

Activity 2: Classifying factory cost centres

Required

Identify from the following examples which cost centres are production cost centres and service cost centres within a clothes manufacturing factory.

	Production cost centre	Service cost centre
Canteen		
Stores		
Stitching		
Maintenance		
Packing		
Finishing		

Key term

Profit centres – similar to cost centres but are accountable for costs and revenues, for example, a sales department in an organisation which earns revenue from sales but incurs costs such as a salesperson's salary and commission.

Revenue centres – similar to cost centres and profit centres but are accountable for revenues only.

Investment centre – a profit centre with additional responsibilities for capital investment. An example might be a separate division of the organisation which has a factory from which it produces goods, sells and despatches them.

Using an example of a solicitors' firm, departments based on their activities (eg corporate law, private client and litigation departments) would be considered profit centres. This is because they incur costs such as the salaries of the solicitors employed in each centre, but also generate income from charging work to clients.

The firm also has service departments such as IT, HR (Personnel), Finance teams etc. These would be considered cost centres, or more specifically, service cost centres, incurring their own costs such as staff salaries but not raising income for the firm.

Let's say the firm had two different offices. One office is in the north and one is in the south of the country. Both offices incur the above costs and generate income, but each office is responsible for the costs of its own building – then the separate offices would each be considered investment centres.

Activity 3: Classifying centres

Required

Suggest what types of centres are appropriate for the following list:

Cost centre	Revenue centre	Profit centre	Investment centre

Factory canteen providing free meals
An independent restaurant
Shop in chain
Car dealer

6 Allocation and apportionment of indirect costs (overheads)

Assessment focus point

While you may be required to answer numerical or descriptive questions on absorption of overheads, there will not be extensive examination of this. This assessment is not aiming specifically to test the absorption of overheads but instead, to test that such activity is a tool in the preparation of budgets.

There are three main methods of calculating a cost per unit. These allocate overheads in different ways. You will have covered these in earlier studies, but we will recap these here:

- **Absorption costing** – a method whereby **all production costs** are included in the costing of a cost unit, ie direct materials, direct labour, variable production overheads and fixed production overheads.

    Note that even when applying absorption costing, it is usually only the production overheads of the production and service cost centres that are absorbed. Administrative overheads (eg the salaries of the finance team, the depreciation of the office building) or selling overheads (eg the cost of an advertising campaign) will remain outside the cost units.

- **Variable or marginal costing** – under this method, only the variable costs of production are included in the cost per unit. The fixed overheads are treated as period costs and not as part of the cost unit. Therefore, a cost unit consists of direct materials, direct labour and variable production overheads.

    The fixed overheads are charged to the statement of profit or loss as an expense for the period.

- **Activity based costing** – this is a method of absorption costing which uses more sophisticated methods of allocating overheads to cost units than the normal methods of overhead allocation and apportionment. It does this by considering the activities that cause the overhead to be incurred and the factors that give rise to the costs (cost drivers).

Activity 4: Absorption costing vs marginal costing

A business expects to produce 5,000 units of its single product in the next month, with the following costs being incurred:

	£
Direct materials	12,000
Direct labour	15,000
Variable overheads	23,000
Fixed overheads	25,000

Required

Complete the following table to show the cost per unit under both absorption costing and marginal costing methods.

Costing method	Cost per unit £
Absorption costing	
Marginal costing	

Illustration 5: Absorption costing vs marginal costing

Fenton Partners produce one product, the Fenton. The factory has two production departments, assembly and packing, and there is one service department, maintenance. Over 75% of the maintenance department's time is spent in the assembly department; and the remainder, in the packing department.

The expected costs of producing 100,000 units in the next quarter are as follows:

Direct materials	£24.00 per unit
Direct labour	2 hours assembly @ £7.00 per hour
	1 hour packing @ £6.00 per hour
Assembly overheads	£320,000
Packing overheads	£240,000
Maintenance overheads	£200,000

In each of the production and service departments, it is estimated that 40% of the overheads are variable and the remainder are fixed. Overheads are absorbed on the basis of labour hours.

Absorption costing

Production overheads

		Assembly £	Packing £	Maintenance £
Allocated and apportioned		320,000	240,000	200,000
Reapportioned – maintenance (75%/25%)		150,000	50,000	(200,000)
Total overhead		470,000	290,000	
Total hours	2 × 100,000	200,000		
	1 × 100,000		100,000	
Absorption rate		470,000	290,000	
		200,000	100,000	
	=	£2.35 per labour hour	£2.90 per labour hour	

Interpretation:

For every one hour that the product is worked on in the assembly department, it is charged with a £2.35 share of the overheads incurred.

For every one hour that the product is worked on in the packing department, it is charged with a £2.90 share of the overheads incurred.

Unit cost

	£
Direct materials	24.00
Direct labour – assembly 2 hours × £7.00	14.00
Direct labour – packing 1 hour × £6.00	6.00
Overheads – assembly 2 hours × £2.35	4.70
– packing 1 hour × £2.90	2.90
Unit cost (total absorption costing)	51.60

Marginal costing

In this method, only variable overheads are included in the cost per unit, so these must be ascertained:

	Assembly	Packing
	£	£
Total overhead	470,000	290,000
Variable element (40%)	188,000	116,000
Absorption rate	188,000	116,000
	200,000	100,000
=	£0.94 per labour hour	£1.16 per labour hour

Unit cost

	£
Direct materials	24.00
Direct labour – assembly	14.00
Direct labour – packing	6.00
Variable overhead – assembly (2 hours × £0.94)	1.88
– packing (1 hour × £1.16)	1.16
Unit cost (marginal costing)	47.04

Selection of appropriate accounting treatment for costs

The example above is comprehensive. You might not be tested on this subject in this manner (ie by having to perform the whole calculation, having been told how overheads are absorbed, but you do need a thorough understanding of the principles as you may be tested on parts of this, or be asked to complete a budget, which we will consider later in this Course Book, based on either marginal or absorption costing).

As an example, you may be asked to select appropriate accounting treatment for various costs in a budget.

Illustration 6: Accounting treatment for costs

Richards Engineering Ltd has the following costs. The appropriate accounting treatment for each of the costs when constructing a budget can be chosen from the list of accounting treatments below.

Costs

Salaries of office staff
Maintenance of machinery
Depreciation of finance director's car
Depreciation of machinery
Packaging material for units of finished goods

List of accounting treatments

Direct cost
Allocate to marketing overheads
Allocate to administrative overheads
Charge to production using a machine hour overhead rate

Salaries of office staff

These are not production costs and so are charged directly to the statement of profit or loss after gross profit ie **allocate to administrative overheads**.

Maintenance of machinery

This is a cost of production and is likely to depend on the use of the machinery, therefore **charge to production using a machine hour overhead rate**.

Depreciation of finance director's car

Allocate to administrative overheads – again, not a production cost. If this had been the sales director's car, then it may have been appropriate to allocate it to marketing overheads.

Depreciation of machinery

This does relate to production, like maintenance of machinery, and **so charge to production using a machine hour overhead rate**.

Packaging material for units of finished goods

This is a raw material cost of production – a **direct cost**.

If you are asked to consider on what basis a production overhead should be absorbed ie on the basis of units, labour hours or machine hours, you need to consider the nature of that specific business.

If the business is labour-intensive, involving many labour hours, then absorption on a labour hour basis is appropriate. Alternatively, if the production process involves the heavy use of machinery, then machine hours would be a more suitable absorption basis.

Activity 5: Identifying accounting treatment for costs

Required

Identify the appropriate accounting treatment for each of the following costs from these options.

Accounting treatment

Direct costs	Allocate to marketing overheads

Allocate to administrative overheads

Charge to production using an overhead absorption rate based on machine hours

Activity based charge to products

Charge to production using an overhead absorption rate based on labour hours

Costs

IT department

Machine maintenance

Sales staff

Supervisors' salaries

Materials used in production

Production workers' salaries

Accounts staff salaries

Production labour – idle time

Purchasing department

6.1 Marginal and absorption costing, inventory levels and profit

Under **absorption costing**, inventory is valued at **full production cost**, which includes the absorbed fixed production overhead.

Under **marginal costing**, the cost per unit only includes variable costs; therefore the value of inventory is lower. Remember also from above that under marginal costing, fixed overheads are charged to the statement of profit or loss as an expense for the period.

Due to the differences in the treatment of fixed overhead and the valuation of inventory, absorption costing and marginal costing will not produce the same profit figure.

An important difference in this context between absorption and marginal costing is that in the marginal costing, we calculate and focus on **contribution** per unit, which is revenue less variable costs per unit.

Activity 6: Inventory levels and profit

Spa Ltd makes a single product and produces management accounts, including a costing statement of profit or loss each month. In both May and June, 100,000 units of the product were produced.

The production costs in both May and June were:

	£
Direct materials	200,000
Direct labour	300,000
Fixed overheads	300,000
Total production costs	800,000

There were no opening inventories at the start of May and all of the production for May was sold. However, in June, only 75,000 units of production were sold, leaving 25,000 units in inventory. Each unit is sold for £10.

Required

Complete the following statements of profit or loss, under absorption and marginal costing principles for the months of May and June.

(a) Absorption costing (AC):

	May		June	
	£	£	£	£
Sales				
Less cost of sales				
Opening inventory				
Cost of production				
100,000 units × £8				
Less closing inventory				
25,000 units × £8				
Cost of sales				
Profit (AC)				

(b) Marginal costing (MC):

	May		June	
	£	£	£	£
Sales				
Less cost of sales				
Opening inventory				
Cost of production				
100,000 units × £5				
Less closing inventory				
25,000 units × £5				
Marginal cost of sales				
Contribution				
Less fixed costs				
Profit (MC)				

6.2 Activity based costing

An alternative method of absorption costing is **activity based costing** (ABC).

The principle of ABC is to break down the overheads into their constituent elements – for example, costs incurred due to receiving materials, costs incurred due to issuing materials to production, costs incurred due to setting up machines for a production run (production setups), costs incurred due to quality control procedures etc.

6.2.1 Cost pools

Each of these elements that cause costs to be incurred are called **activities** and the costs associated with each activity are gathered together into **cost pools**. For each cost pool, what must then be identified is the factor that causes or drives these costs to change. This is known as the **cost driver**.

The total of the cost pool is then divided by the number of times the cost driver takes place and this gives an overhead rate per cost driver. The overheads from the cost pool are then allocated to different products, depending upon their particular usage of the cost driver.

The diagram that follows illustrates in outline how ABC works:

Identify activities causing overheads	Activity 1	Activity 2
Gather all costs for each activity	Cost pool 1	Cost pool 2
Identify what causes the cost	Cost driver 1	Cost driver 2
Calculate cost driver rate	Cost pool 1 total / No. of cost drivers	Cost pool 2 total / No. of cost drivers
Apply to individual cost units	Use of cost driver × cost driver rate	Use of cost driver × cost driver rate

Illustration 7: Activity based costing

KPL Ltd produces two products, the C and the P. The direct costs per unit of the two products are given below:

	C	P
Direct materials	£3.50	£4.80
Direct labour	£2.00	£1.20

The budgeted production is for 120,000 units of C and 50,000 units of P.

The two main activities identified for the fairly simple production process are materials handling and production setups.

C requires only large production runs and large transfers of materials from stores. However, P is a more complex product, with a number of different types of materials required; and shorter and more frequent production runs.

The budgeted overheads for KPL are £800,000 and they are made up as follows:

	£
Materials handling cost pool	300,000
Production setup cost pool	500,000
	800,000

The use of these activities for each product is as follows:

	C	P	Total
Number of materials requisitions	200	800	1,000
Number of production setups	100	400	500

Calculate the total costs incurred and the unit cost of each product using the costing method of activity based costing. Also calculate the direct cost and the overhead cost per unit.

Cost driver rate

Materials handling	$\dfrac{£300,000}{1,000}$	=	£300 per materials requisition
Production setups	$\dfrac{£500,000}{500}$	=	£1,000 per production setup

Total production costs and cost per unit

	C £	P £
Direct materials		
120,000 × £3.50	420,000	
50,000 × £4.80		240,000
Direct labour		
120,000 × £2.00	240,000	
50,000 × £1.20		60,000
Materials handling overhead		
200 × £300	60,000	
800 × £300		240,000
Production setup overhead		
100 × £1,000	100,000	
400 × £1,000		400,000
	820,000	940,000
Cost per unit	£820,000 / 120,000 units	£940,000 / 50,000 units
	£6.83 per unit	£18.80 per unit

Analysis of cost per unit

		C £	P £
Direct costs	(3.50 + 2.00)	5.50	
	(4.80 + 1.20)		6.00
Materials handling overhead			
60,000/120,000		0.50	
240,000/50,000			4.80
Production setup overhead			
100,000/120,000		0.83	
400,000/50,000			8.00
Unit cost		6.83	18.80

In this instance, C is charged with £0.50 + £0.83 = £1.33 of production overhead, whereas the more activity-intensive P is charged with £12.80 of production overhead. Given that the direct labour cost of product P is only £1.20 compared to the £2.00 labour cost of C, if the overheads had been apportioned according to labour hours, as with traditional absorption costing, then the picture would have been very different indeed.

Activity 7: Activity based costing

The costs of the quality control department of a manufacturing business are estimated to be £74,000 for the next quarter. During that period, it is estimated that there will be 370 quality inspections. Product A will require 25 inspections during the quarter; and Product B, 130 inspections.

Required

Using activity based costing, how much quality control overhead will be absorbed into Product A and Product B?

Overhead included in Product A	
Overhead included in Product B	

Chapter summary

- The nature of costs must be determined before budgets can be constructed.

- Costs are often classified according to their behaviour as activity levels change – the main classifications are variable costs, fixed costs, stepped costs and semi-variable costs.

- Costs are either capital or revenue in nature. Revenue expenditure is included in the cost of a product, but capital expenditure is not. Capital expenditure is converted to revenue expenditure in the form of depreciation.

- Direct costs are costs that can be related directly to a cost unit, whereas indirect costs (or overheads) cannot be attributed directly to a cost unit and instead are initially allocated or apportioned to a cost centre.

- Different departments or functions can be classified, according to responsibility, as profit centres, investment centres or cost centres.

- These responsibility centres each have a budget associated with them which are combined to form the budget of an organisation.

- Costs must be allocated and attributed to the relevant responsibility centre.

- There are three main methods of attributing indirect costs to production units – absorption costing, marginal costing and activity based costing (ABC).

- Absorption costing is where the production overheads are included in the cost of each cost unit.

- Under marginal costing, only variable overheads are included in the cost of cost units, with the fixed overheads being charged to the statement of profit or loss as a period cost.

- Activity based costing (ABC) considers the activities that cause overheads to be incurred and the factors that give rise to costs (cost drivers). It is a method of absorbing overheads into products on the basis of the amount of each activity that the particular product is expected to use in the period.

Keywords

- **Absorption costing:** a costing method which includes all production overheads within the cost of the cost units

- **Activity based costing:** a more complex approach to absorption of overheads, based upon analysis of the detailed causes of overheads

- **Budget:** a formalised, numerical plan of action for a business

- **Capital expenditure:** purchases of non-current assets or the improvement of the earning capability of non-current assets

- **Cost centre:** an area of the business for which costs are incurred

- **Cost unit:** in a manufacturing business, each unit of production; in service industries such as hospitality, it may be, for example, each meal served

- **Direct cost:** cost that can be directly attributed to a cost unit

- **Fixed cost:** cost that remains constant as activity levels change

- **Full production cost:** prime cost plus indirect costs of production

- **Indirect cost (overhead):** cost that cannot be attributed directly to a cost unit

- **Investment centre:** an area which incurs costs, generates income but also accounts for its own capital employed

- **Marginal costing:** a costing method which includes only variable costs within the cost of the cost units with fixed costs written off as period costs

- **Prime cost:** the total of all direct costs

- **Profit centre:** an area of the business which incurs costs, but also generates income

- **Relevant range:** the range of activity levels over which a fixed cost will not change

- **Revenue expenditure:**
  - Purchase of goods for resale
  - Maintenance of the existing earning capacity of non-current assets
  - Expenditure incurred in conducting the business

- **Semi-variable cost:** cost which has both a fixed element and variable element

- **Stepped cost:** cost which is fixed over a relatively short range and then increases in steps

- **Variable cost:** cost that increases/decreases directly in line with any change in activity level

Activity answers

Activity 1: High-low calculation

	Output	Cost
Highest	14,000	35,000
Lowest	10,000	27,000
	4,000	8,000

$\therefore$ VC/unit = £8,000 / 4,000 = £2

Total costs	35,000
Variable cost	(28,000)
$\therefore$ Fixed cost	7,000

Activity 2: Classifying factory cost centres

Production cost centre	Service cost centre
Packing	Canteen
Finishing	Stores
Stitching	Maintenance

Activity 3: Classifying centres

Factory canteen providing free meals – Cost centre

Car dealer – Revenue centre

Shop in chain – Profit centre

An independent restaurant – Investment centre

Activity 4: Absorption costing vs marginal costing

Costing method	Cost per unit £
Absorption costing	15.00
Marginal costing	10.00

Cost per unit – absorption costing

		£
Direct materials		12,000
Direct labour		15,000
Variable overheads		23,000
Fixed overheads		<u>25,000</u>
Total cost		<u>75,000</u>
Cost per unit	=	£75,000/5,000
	=	£15 per unit

Cost per unit – marginal costing

		£
Direct materials		12,000
Direct labour		15,000
Variable overheads		<u>23,000</u>
Total cost		<u>50,000</u>
Cost per unit	=	£50,000/5,000
	=	£10 per unit

Activity 5: Identifying accounting treatment for costs

Costs	Accounting treatment
IT department	Allocate to administrative overheads
Machine maintenance	Charge to production using an overhead absorption rate based on machine hours
Sales staff	Allocate to marketing overheads
Supervisors' salaries	Charge to production using an overhead absorption rate based on labour hours
Materials used in production	Direct cost
Production workers' salaries	Direct cost
Accounts staff salaries	Allocate to administrative overheads
Production labour idle time	Charge to production using an overhead absorption rate based on labour hours
Purchasing department	Activity based charge to products

Activity 6: Inventory levels and profit

Statements of profit or loss

(a) Absorption costing:

Unit cost

£800,000/100,000 = £8 per unit

	May £	May £	June £	June £
Sales		1,000,000		750,000
Less cost of sales				
Opening inventory	–		–	
Cost of production				
100,000 units × £8	800,000		800,000	
	800,000		800,000	
Less closing inventory				
25,000 units × £8	–		(200,000)	
Cost of sales		800,000		600,000
Profit (AC)		200,000		150,000

(b) Marginal costing:

Unit cost

£500,000/100,000 = £5 per unit

	May £	May £	June £	June £
Sales		1,000,000		750,000
Less cost of sales				
Opening inventory	–			
Cost of production				
100,000 units × £5	500,000		500,000	
	500,000		500,000	
Less closing inventory				
25,000 units × £5	–	–	(125,000)	
Marginal cost of sales		500,000		375,000
Contribution		500,000		375,000
Less fixed costs		300,000		300,000
Profit (MC)		200,000		75,000

In May, the profit is the same under both costing methods – £200,000. This is because there is no movement in inventory during the period, since all of the production is sold.

In June, however, profit under absorption costing is £150,000, whereas it is only £75,000 under the marginal costing method. The reason for the £75,000 difference in profit is that the closing inventory, under absorption costing, includes £75,000 (£300,000/100,000 × 25,000 units) of fixed costs that are being carried forward to the next accounting period, whereas under marginal costing, they were all written off in June.

The rules are that:

(1) **If inventory levels are rising, then absorption costing will give higher profits** (as the fixed overheads are being carried forward into the next accounting period).

(2) **If inventory levels are falling, then absorption costing will give a lower profit figure** (as more fixed overheads from the previous period are charged to the statement of profit or loss in this period).

(3) **Where inventory levels are constant (provided that unit costs are constant), then absorption costing and marginal costing will give the same level of profit.**

Activity 7: Activity based costing

Overhead included in Product A	£5,000
Overhead included in Product B	£26,000

Cost per inspection	=	£74,000/370
	=	£200 per inspection
Overhead included in A's cost	=	£200 × 25
	=	£5,000
Overhead included in B's cost	=	£200 × 130
	=	£26,000

Test your learning

1   **To which responsibility centre should these costs be allocated? Choose from the list below.**

    Costs:

    Overtime costs of production workers
    Depreciation of cars used by sales staff
    Training course for sales director
    Advertising posters

    Responsibility centres:

    HR (Personnel) department
    Sales department
    Marketing department
    Production department

2   An organisation pays for annual computer support from an external firm. This costs £2,000 per annum plus £100 for each computer used in the company.

    The cost behaviour demonstrated by this cost is [▼]

    Picklist:

    fixed
    semi-variable
    stepped
    variable

3   A manufacturing company budgets for one supervisor at a cost of £20,000 for every 100,000 units produced annually. The company expects to make 270,000 units in the coming year.

    The budgeted cost for supervisors is £ [   ]

    This cost exhibits [▼] behaviour

    Picklist:

    semi-variable
    stepped
    variable

4   The direct materials cost for 10,000 units is estimated to be £43,600; and for 12,000, it is estimated to be £52,320.

    This a purely variable cost. True or false?

5   A business expects to incur fixed costs of £64,000 in the next month. **What are the budgeted total fixed cost and the budgeted fixed cost per unit if activity levels are:**

	Fixed costs (£)	Cost per unit (£ to nearest 1p)
(a) 3,000 units?		
(b) 10,000 units?		
(c) 16,000 units?		

6   **Select an appropriate accounting treatment for each of the following costs:**

Cost of the production staff canteen ▼

Redecorating reception area ▼

Machine maintenance ▼

Sick pay for production workers ▼

Picklist for line items:

Activity based charge to production cost centres
Allocate to administrative overheads
Charge to production in a labour hour overhead rate
Charge to production in a machine hour overhead rate

7   A department has the following indirect costs in its annual budget.

	£
Management salaries	55,000
Depreciation	26,000
Heat, power and water	85,000
Machine maintenance	14,000
Total	180,000

The budgeted production is 6,000 units, which will require 30,000 machine hours and 5,000 direct labour hours.

How should the indirect costs be absorbed (labour hours, machine hours or units produced), and what is the absorption rate?

8   A business produces two products, the GH and the JK. There are two production cost centres, cutting and finishing, and one service cost centre, stores. It is estimated that 80% of the stores activity is for the cutting cost centre.

The expected costs for the next quarter for production are:

Direct materials –	GH	£20.00 per unit
	JK	£12.00 per unit
Direct labour –	GH – cutting	3 hours @ £8.00 per hour
	GH – finishing	1 hour @ £6.40 per hour
	JK – cutting	2 hours @ £8.00 per hour
	JK – finishing	0.5 hours @ £6.40
Cutting overheads		£225,000
Finishing overheads		£180,000
Stores overheads		£100,000

All overhead costs are expected to be fixed costs.

It is budgeted that 50,000 units of GH and 30,000 units of JK will be produced during the quarter.

The budget is to be constructed using total absorption costing.

Complete the following table:

	Cutting	Finishing
Re-apportioned store overheads (£)		
Overhead absorption rate		

Costs per unit	GH (£)	JK (£)
Direct materials		
Direct labour		
Overheads		
Total cost per unit		

9   A business produces two products, the LM and the NP. The direct costs of the two products are:

	LM	NP
Direct materials	£2.60	£3.90
Direct labour	£3.50	£2.70

The total overhead cost is made up as follows:

	£
Stores costs	140,000
Production setup costs	280,000
Quality control inspection costs	180,000
	600,000

The budgeted production is for 50,000 units of LM and 20,000 units of NP.

Each product is expected to make the following use of the service activities:

	LM	NP	Total
Materials requisitions	100	220	320
Production setups	80	200	280
Quality control inspections	30	60	90

Complete the following:

Overheads should be absorbed on an activity basis as follows:

Stores costs = £ ☐ per ☐

Production setup costs = £ ☐ per ☐

Quality control costs = £ ☐ per ☐

The budgeted cost per unit of LM is £ ☐

The budgeted cost per unit of NP is £ ☐

Forecasting data

2

Learning outcomes

1.1	**Identify internal and external sources of information used to forecast income and expenditure** • Select the appropriate sources of data to use for forecasting • Describe their sources of data when issuing forecast

1.2	**Use statistical techniques to forecast income and expenditure**
	
	• Apply the following techniques
	
	    – Sampling
	    – Indices
	    – Time series; trends and seasonal variation

1.3	**Discuss the purpose of revenue and cost forecasts and their link to budgets** • Differentiate between forecasts and plans • Describe how each forecast contributes to the budgeting process • Describe the methods of dealing with the uncertainty inherent in forecasting (planning models, regular reforecasting, rebudgeting, rolling budgets and budget flexing)
1.4	**Identify the impact of internal and external factors on income and expenditure forecasts** • Advise on the reliability of forecasts • Describe the stages and features of the product life cycle and their impact on income forecasts • Describe market trends and competitive pressures • Explain the expected impact of promotional activity • Identify and describe external events affecting the reliability of cost forecasts
2.1	**Identify budgetary responsibilities and accountabilities** • Select the appropriate managers to provide information required to prepare budgets

Assessment context

You could be required to forecast figures for inclusion in budgets.

Qualification context

Forecasting techniques are tested in *Management Accounting: Budgeting* and *Management Accounting: Decision and Control* at Level 4.

Business context

Business will use a variety of models and techniques to help them forecast the performance of their business.

Chapter overview

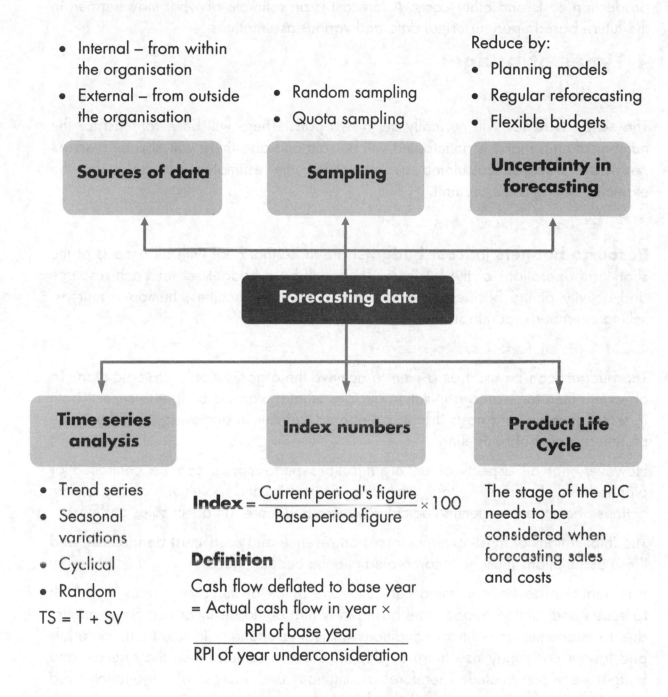

- Internal – from within the organisation
- External – from outside the organisation

- Random sampling
- Quota sampling

Reduce by:
- Planning models
- Regular reforecasting
- Flexible budgets

Sources of data

Sampling

Uncertainty in forecasting

Forecasting data

Time series analysis

Index numbers

Product Life Cycle

- Trend series
- Seasonal variations
- Cyclical
- Random

TS = T + SV

$$\text{Index} = \frac{\text{Current period's figure}}{\text{Base period figure}} \times 100$$

Definition

Cash flow deflated to base year
= Actual cash flow in year × $\dfrac{\text{RPI of base year}}{\text{RPI of year underconsideration}}$

The stage of the PLC needs to be considered when forecasting sales and costs

Introduction

In order to prepare budgets, any business will need to produce forecasts of its sales, production costs and other costs. A forecast is an estimate of what may happen in the future based upon historical data and various assumptions.

1 Types of budget

1.1 Sales budget

The **sales budget** will normally be in two parts. There will be a forecast for the number of units that it is anticipated will be sold and also there will also be a **sales revenue budget** calculated by multiplying the estimated unit sales by the expected selling price per unit.

1.2 Resource budgets

Resource budgets (or **cost budgets**) are those that deal with all aspects of the short-term operations of the business. There will be a budget set for each resource and activity of the business – production, production facilities, human resources, selling overheads, administration etc.

1.2.1 Link of forecasts to budgets

The budgets can be used as a plan to achieve the organisation's strategic plan. To an extent therefore, an organisation decides what it wants a budget to reflect, both in terms of sales, and costs that it is prepared to incur in achieving this. This is the planning aspect of budgeting.

However, not all aspects of an organisations performance can be controlled or planned for. External factors, including economic and political conditions, the actions of competitors, technological advances and more, all affect sales and costs.

The implications of these external forces on revenue and costs must be forecast, and these assumptions must be incorporated into the budget figures.

It is important to bear in mind here that one or all of the assumptions on which forecasts and related budgets are based may turn out to be incorrect. For example, due to economic or political conditions (including changes in taxation), materials and labour costs may rise more quickly than was assumed when the forecast and budget were constructed. Therefore, assumptions and sources of information used when creating forecasts and budgets should always be documented so that anyone using them is aware of the risks and uncertainties involved.

Forecasts and budgets should be updated when necessary to take account of new relevant information, such as changes in inflation or increases/decreases in predicted sales demand. Regular reforecasting and rebudgeting can help to mitigate the inherent risks relating to the assumptions made when budgeting.

1.3 Forecasts and plans

Although the words are often used interchangeably, there is a distinction in budgeting between a **forecast** and a **plan**.

A forecast is no more than an expectation or estimate of what might happen in the future based on historical data and analysis using various assumptions, whereas a plan is a deliberate commitment or intent.

A budget is a plan but it takes into account forecasts of factors over which the organisation does not have control. When preparing budgets, it is important to distinguish which factors are under the control of the organisation; and which are outside its control, and so have to be managed.

The data required to prepare forecasts and forecasting techniques will be considered later in this chapter.

2 Sources of data

Data required for forecasting may be obtained from either an internal source or from an external source. Note that in this Course Book, we will use the terms data and information interchangeably, although technically, data is unprocessed facts and figures, and information is data that has been processed into a useable form.

2.1 Internal data

Key term

Internal data – data collected from internal documents or sources.

These could include: financial accounting records, purchase invoices, payroll information, sales information, inventory records, production information, published accounts and historical records.

2.2 External data

Key term

External data – data collected from sources outside the business.

These could include: the internet, market research, interviews, online questionnaires (primary external data), government statistics eg RPI, national statistics, banks, newspapers, trade journals, reference manuals, consultancies, libraries, advice and information bureaux.

2.3 Limitations of secondary external sources of data

Secondary external sources of data have four limitations:

- Users will be unaware of any limitations in the data
- Data may not be suitable for the purpose it is being used for
- It may be out-of-date
- The geographical area covered may not be appropriate

Examples include: government statistics, banks, financial newspapers, trade journals, libraries, and the internet.

2.4 Key budget factor

The forecast of the **key budget factor** should be made first. The **key budget factor** is the element or resource of the business that is likely to be the one that

places limitations on the activities of the business. It is also known as the **limiting factor**. (We will look other limiting factors in a later chapter.)

In most businesses, the key budget factor will be sales. Most businesses will find that there is a limit to the amount of sales that they can make due to demand for their products and their own market share. However, it is also possible that the key budget factor may be the availability of materials.

Once the key budget factor has been identified, then the budget for this factor can be set. If sales are the key budget factor, then the sales quantity forecast must be made first. This can then be used to determine the amount of the product that must be produced each period in the production budget and from this, the other resource budgets can follow.

Alternatively, if the key budget factor is, for example, machine capacity, then the machine hours usage budget must be set first, which will then determine the maximum production for each period on which the other resource budgets can be based.

2.5 Forecasting sales

There are a number of methods that can be used when forecasting sales. These can include:

- Knowledge of sales experts within the business – for example, the impact of market trends, promotional activity etc

- Market research and sampling

- Time series analysis – moving averages, trend and seasonal variations

- Product life cycle analysis and market knowledge

- Index numbers

2.6 Forecasting expenditure

There are a number of methods that can be used when forecasting expenditure. These can include:

- Knowledge of purchasing managers
- Knowledge of production managers
- Market research and sampling
- Time series analysis – moving averages, trend and seasonal variations
- Index numbers

Activity 1: Sources of information

Identify the sources you would use to obtain information on the following items.

Information required	Source
Inflation	Market research
Sales demand	National Statistics Office
Competitor wage rates	Bank
Employment data	Stock listing in financial press
Cost of finance	Trade association
Share prices	

Activity 2: Sources of information 2

You are constructing a budget and require the following pieces of information. Select which source you could use to find the appropriate information.

Information required	Source
Population figures for areas in the UK	HM Revenue & Customs
VAT rates	Financial Times newspaper
Possible sales prices achievable in the market place	Office for National Statistics
	Trade journal
	Purchasing manager

2.7 Contacts for information

As a budget accountant, you will also need to contact various people or groups within the organisation for different tasks within the budgeting process.

Activity 3: Contacts for information

Required

Identify the contact you would use in the following scenarios from the given options:

Task	Contact
Forecasting the labour rate for next year	Production manager
Reviewing the budget	Budget committee
Forecasting the quantity of materials per unit for next year	HR manager
Preparing the advertising budget	Marketing director
	Buyer

Illustration 1: Direct labour budget

The finance manager is pulling together the budget for next year for direct labour.

The labour cost for the current year is forecast to be £300,000.

The production manager has forecast that the labour force will need to increase by 2%. The personnel manager has advised that all staff will receive a 3% wage increase from the start of the next financial year.

Calculate how much the direct labour budget should be.

The direct labour budget should be £315,180

$300,000 \times 1.02 \times 1.03 = £315,180$

Activity 4: Materials budget

The finance manager has put together the materials budget based upon a 5% increase in volume and a 4% increase in prices. This resulted in a budgeted material cost of £520,000.

The purchasing manager has now advised that after negotiations with suppliers, prices should not be budgeted to rise by 4% but instead, will remain constant.

Required

Calculate how much the revised materials budget should be.

The materials budget should be £ [   ]

3 Time series analysis

Key term

Time series analysis – a series of figures or values recorded over time.

Time series analysis is an analysis of past patterns of demand or sales which will be used to construct expected patterns in the future. For example:

* Output at a factory each day for the last month
* Total costs per annum for last ten years
* Monthly sales over last five years

3.1 Components of a time series (TS)

Trend (T)

(a) General movement of a **time series** over a long period of time (ie growth, inflation)

(b) Generally expected to be a smooth line/curve

(c) Find by method of moving averages

For example, a steady decline in the average sales of a national daily newspaper or a steady increase in sales of the Sony PlayStation 3.

Seasonal variations (SV)

A predicted movement away from the trend due to repetitive events over a short, but fixed, period of time (weekly, quarterly).

For example, sales of tabloid newspapers being higher on Mondays and Saturdays than other days due to the extra sports coverage, or sales of ice cream being higher in summer than in winter.

Cyclical variations (C)

Recurring patterns over a longer period of time, not generally of a fixed nature (ie recession/depression/economic growth).

For example, changes in unemployment, movement from recession to economic growth.

Random variations (R)

Irregular/unpredictable variations, due to rare/chance occurrences (hurricanes, floods, nuclear war).

For example, high sales of a tabloid newspaper due to exclusive photographs of a member of the royal family.

3.2 The additive model

This is where the components are assumed to add together to give the forecast sales.

$$TS = T + SV + R + C$$

Where:

TS = Time series forecast

T = Trend

SV = Seasonal variations

R = Random variations

C = Cyclical variations

In the exam, students will only be required to deal with the trend and seasonal variations in calculations. So the formula becomes:

 Formula to learn

TS = T + SV

The seasonal variations in time series analysis can be expressed as additions to, or subtractions from, the trend.

3.3 Moving averages

The main method for calculating a trend from a time series is the technique of **moving averages**, which is an average of the results of a fixed number of periods and relates to the mid-point of the overall period.

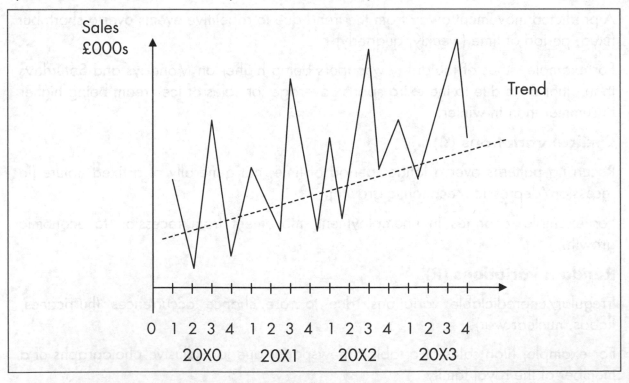

In the above example, there would appear to be a large seasonal variation in demand, but there is also a basic upward trend.

Illustration 2: Moving averages

Suppose that the sales figures for a business for the first six months of the year are as follows:

	£
January	35,500
February	37,500
March	34,500
April	40,000
May	42,000
June	39,000

It is felt that the sales cycle changes on a quarterly basis – ie the seasonal variations repeat themselves every three months. What is required, therefore, is a three month moving average. This is done by first totalling the figures for January, February and March and then finding the average:

$$\frac{35,500 + 37,500 + 34,500}{3} = £35,833$$

Then we move on by one month, and the average for February, March and April sales is calculated:

$$\frac{37,500 + 34,500 + 40,000}{3} = £37,333$$

Then, the average for March, April and May would be calculated as follows:

$$\frac{34,500 + 40,000 + 42,000}{3} = £38,833$$

Finally the average for April, May and June can be determined:

$$\frac{40,000 + 42,000 + 39,000}{3} = £40,333$$

Now we can show these moving averages, together with the original figures – the convention is to show the moving average next to the middle month of those used in the average.

	Actual data £	Moving average – Trend £	Seasonal variation £
January	35,500		
February	37,500	35,833	+1,667
March	34,500	37,333	-2,833
April	40,000	38,833	+1,167
May	42,000	40,333	+1,667
June	39,000		

3.4 Calculating forecast sales using the additive model

Once the trend has been established, the forecast sales can be determined.

> **Formula to learn**
>
> Additive model: TS = T + SV

Activity 5: The additive model – YSP Games Ltd

You are employed as an accounting technician at YSP Games Ltd.

The market research department has gathered information about the typical trend and seasonal variation for sales volumes for the year ended November 20X7. This information is produced below.

Month	Dec	Jan	Feb	Mar	Apr	May	Jun	Jul	Aug	Sept	Oct	Nov
Trend ('000)	250	255	260	265	270	275	280	285	290	295	300	305
SV ('000)												
Actual volume of sales ('000)	600	55	50	115	140	175	220	285	290	445	475	480

Required

(a) Explain the terms 'trend' and 'seasonal variation'.

(b) Complete the table above, by calculating the seasonal variation for 20X7.

(c) Using the information in the table above, calculate the forecast sales volumes per month for the period August 20X8 to December 20X8.

Month	Aug X8	Sept X8	Oct X8	Nov X8	Dec X8
Trend ('000)					
SV ('000)					
Forecast sales volume ('000)					

48

BPP
LEARNING MEDIA

Activity 6: The additive model 2

This year, sales are £400,000. Analysis of recent years' sales shows a growth trend of 6% per year.

The seasonal variation has been:

Quarter 1	−£8,000
Quarter 2	−£1,000
Quarter 3	−£2,000
Quarter 4	+£11,000

Required

Forecast the sales revenue for each quarter of next year.

Quarter	Underlying trend £	Seasonal Variation £	Forecast £
1			
2			
3			
4			
Year			

3.5 The multiplicative model

The seasonal variations in time series analysis can also be shown as percentages of the trend in the multiplicative model:

Illustration 3: Multiplicative model

The trend figures for sales in units for Earthware Design for the four quarters of 20X0 are given below:

Quarter 1	158,400
Quarter 2	159,900
Quarter 3	161,500
Quarter 4	163,100

The seasonal variations are expressed as follows:

Quarter 1	+8%
Quarter 2	–5%
Quarter 3	–17%
Quarter 4	+14%

What are the forecast sales for each of the quarters of 20X0?

Quarter 1	158,400 × 1.08	=	171,072
Quarter 2	159,900 × 0.95	=	151,905
Quarter 3	161,500 × 0.83	=	134,045
Quarter 4	163,100 × 1.14	=	185,934

3.6 Forecasting problems

Whilst time series analysis has the advantage of being simple to calculate and is useful for identifying an underlying pattern, it suffers from forecasting problems.

- The further into the future, the more unreliable the trend
- Pattern of trend and seasonal variations may not continue
- Random variations may upset trends
- Environmental changes
- Technological changes

4 Index numbers

Index numbers – an index measures the average changes in the values, prices or quantities of a group of items over time.

An index can either be a price or a quantity index for an item or a group of items.

4.1 Characteristics

- Base year – a point in time with which current prices/quantities are compared.
- Weightings are used and they give the relative importance of each item.
- Index numbers may be used to deflate costs for comparison.

4.2 Retail price index (RPI) or cost of living index

The **retail price index** measures the changes in the costs of items of expenditure of the average household.

It can also be used to deflate time-related data (covered later in this chapter).

4.3 Limitations of index numbers

Decisions need to be made regarding the following.

- What items to select for a 'basket'?

- What weightings to use to reflect performance?

- How to determine a 'typical' base year?

- New products or items may appear; old ones might get discontinued. Hence, the index needs to be regularly revised.

- How to source the data and determine its accuracy?

We can get a feel for how data is moving over time by converting the actual figures into a series of index numbers.

This is done by, firstly, determining a **base period**, which is the period for which the actual figure is equated to an index of 100.

Formula to learn

Each subsequent periodic figure is converted to the equivalent index using the following formula:

$$\text{Index} = \frac{\text{Current period's figure}}{\text{Base period figure}} \times 100$$

4.4 Interpreting an index

If the index for a period is greater than 100, this means that the current period figure is larger than the base period figure. If it is less than 100, the figure is lower than the base period figure. If the index is generally rising, then the figures are

increasing over the base period; but if the index is decreasing, the figures are decreasing in comparison to the base period.

Remember when interpreting an index, that it represents the current period figure compared to the base period – not compared to the previous period.

4.5 Usefulness of indexation in forecasting

Like time series analysis, indexing is another technique for analysing figures for income (or cost) collected over a period of time. From this, management have a greater awareness of the trend of this income, and by extrapolating this trend, sales forecasts can be produced.

As with time series analysis, however, the trend will not continue indefinitely into the future, and external factors regarding the product's market and also its life cycle, should also be taken into account.

Activity 7: Index numbers 1

The cost per kg for the materials used in production has been as follows for the last four months.

January X8	February X8	March X8	April X8
£26.20	£26.80	£26.90	£25.80

Required

(a) **Convert the costs per kg for January to April into index numbers using January 20X7 as the base period. The price per kg at January 20X7 was £24.95.**

Jan X8 = [ ]

Feb X8 = [ ]

Mar X8 = [ ]

Apr X8 = [ ]

(b) **It is expected that the index number in January 20X9 will be 108.26. Calculate the expected cost per kg for January 20X9.**

Expected cost = [ ] per kg

(c) **Calculate the percentage increase in the price of materials from January 20X7 to January 20X9.**

Percentage increase = [ ] %

Note. Round answers to 2dp.

Activity 8: Index numbers 2 – JB Ltd

JB Ltd is planning ahead and wishes to forecast the cost of its main ingredient used in the manufacture of product X.

Required

(a) **Complete the table to show the underlying cost and the forecast cost for each of the months April to June.**

Month	Jan	Feb	Mar	Apr	May	Jun
Underlying cost per kg (£)	180	210	240			
Seasonal variation (£)	40	12	-18	-8	15	-4
Actual cost/forecast cost (£)	220	222	222			

(b) **The cost per unit of its other key material – BR3 was £50 per kilogram on 1 January X1 and is £80 per kilogram on 1 January X8.**

Using January X1 as the base year, the cost index for material BR3 as at 1 January X8 is ▢ **.**

The cost per unit has increased by ▢ **% between January X1 and X8.**

4.6 Indexation with two variables

If sales are increasing based on a change in sales volume as well as a change in sales price, indices for the two variables can be used to determine the forecasted revenue.

Illustration 4: Indices with two variables.

Mantle Ltd, has actual sales in Year 1 of £275,000. Sales revenue is forecast to increase based on changes in price and changes in volume.

The following indices are available for sales volume and sales price.

	Year 1	Year 2	Year 3	Year 4	Year 5
Sales volume index	120.0	127.0	132.6	144.4	150.0
Sales price index	110.0	115.0	120.0	125.0	130.0

Step 1

Using the sales volume index we can calculate the growth in sales based on the volume increase only, using the following formula:

Current period figure = Base period figure $\times \left(\dfrac{\textbf{current year index}}{\textbf{base year index}} \right)$

So, forecast sales at year 1 prices:

Year 2	£275,000 × (127.0/120.0) = £291,042
Year 3	£275,000 × (132.6/120.0) = £303,875
Year 4	£275,000 × (144.4/120.0) = £330,917
Year 5	£275,000 × (150.0/120.0) = £343,750

Step 2

Using the sales price index we can use the results from Step 1 above to calculate the overall growth in sales revenue, using the following formula:

Current period figure = Base period figure $\times \left(\dfrac{\textbf{current year index}}{\textbf{base year index}} \right)$

So, forecast sales at expected prices:

Year 2	£291,040 × (115.0/110.0) = £304,269
Year 3	£303,875 × (120.0/110.0) = £331,500
Year 4	£330,917 × (125.0/110.0) = £376,042
Year 5	£343,750 × (130.0/110.0) = £406,250

4.7 Time related data and indices

An index can be used to deflate or inflate time-related data, such as wages, to see whether the data in question is rising faster or slower than prices.

4.7.1 Deflation

Formula to learn

| Cash flow deflated to base year | = | Actual cash flow in year under consideration | × | $\dfrac{\text{RPI of base year}}{\text{RPI of year under consideration}}$ |

4.7.2 Inflation

Formula to learn

| Cash flow inflated to the current year | = | Actual cash flow in year under consideration | × | $\dfrac{\text{RPI in current year}}{\text{RPI of year under consideration}}$ |

4.8 Forward Contracts

Key term

Forward Contracts – Forward contracts can be used to protect against rising prices and to try to reduce the risk a company is facing. A contract can be entered into now to agree a price for a certain quantity of items in the future.

Activity 9: Index numbers 3 – Tees R Us

Tees R Us Ltd makes and packs tea bags. The tea is imported from India and the historical cost per kilogram is shown below.

June X7	July X7	Aug X7	Sept X7	Oct X7	Nov X7
£4.95	£4.97	£4.99	£5.05	£5.08	£5.10

Required

(a) **Convert the costs per kg for June and November into index numbers using January 20X7 as the base period. The price per kg at January 20X7 was £4.80.**

(b) **It is expected that the index number for tea in January 20X8 will be 108.25. Calculate the expected cost per kg for January 20X8.**

(c) **Calculate the percentage increase in the price of tea from January 20X7 to January 20X8.**

Activity 10: Forward contracts – Ashby Ltd

Ashby Ltd uses a raw material, ZZ20, in its production. The industry maintains a price index for ZZ20. The index for May 20X9 was 107 and the actual price per tonne was £800. The forecast index for the three months ending November 20X9 is shown below.

Month	September	October	November
Underlying trend in index	110	115	120
Seasonal variation in index	+12	–9	+5
Seasonally adjusted Index	122	106	125

Required

(a) Calculate the expected cost of one tonne of ZZ20 for each of the three months.

(b) The company is able to secure a forward contract price for 80 tonnes of ZZ20 per month for the three months at a price of £900 per tonne. Calculate whether the contract would result in a lower price.

5 Product life cycle

Key term

Product life cycle – many of the forecasting techniques we have looked at assume that sales figures will continue to change in line with a trend. However, this may not always be the case, as products will have different sales and profitability trends, depending on the stage of the product life cycle they are in.

The product life cycle (PLC), developed by Raymond Vernon in 1966, can be divided into five stages.

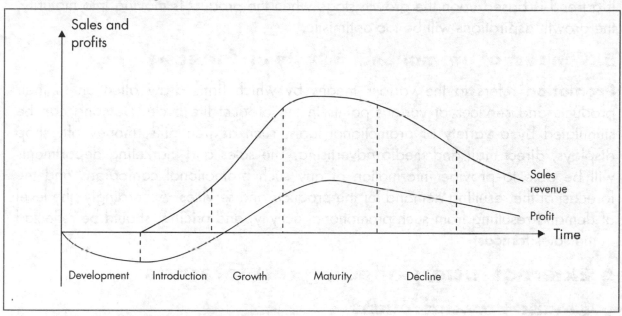

5.1 Characteristics of the PLC

Development
- High capital expenditure
- High R&D

Introduction
- Product introduced
- High capital expenditure
- Initial demand low
- High advertising

Growth
- Increased demand
- Increased revenue
- Profitable
- Product recognition

Maturity
- Growth in demand slows down
- Economies of scale achieved
- Processes automated
- Still profitable
- Product modification to sustain demand

BPP
LEARNING MEDIA

Saturation and Decline

- Demand falls
- Product still profitable until eventually a loss maker
- Product life cycle eventually ends

5.2 Impact of the PLC on forecasts

Clearly the stage of the PLC needs to be taken into account when forecasting future demand.

If a trend is based upon the growth stage when the product is moving into maturity, the growth aspirations will be too optimistic.

5.3 Impact of promotional activity on forecasts

Promotion refers to the various means by which firms draw attention to their products and services at various points in the product life cycle. Demand can be stimulated by a variety of promotional tools, such as free gifts, money off, shop displays, direct mail and media advertising. The sales and marketing departments will be able to provide information of any such promotional campaigns and the forecast of the resulting demand for the products and services. Accordingly, the level of demand resulting from such promotional activity, and pricing, should be reflected in the sales forecast.

6 External factors affecting cost forecasts

6.1 Market considerations

In addition to considering where the individual products of a business are in their life cycle when producing sales forecasts, it is also important to consider the overall market for a particular product. Is it a new, emerging market for a new product, an established market for a long-standing product, or a declining market for a product which is no longer of great interest to consumers?

For example, no matter how technologically advanced a DVD player is, online streaming and other on-demand TV and movie services, mean that demand for DVD players is in terminal decline.

Furthermore, the level of competition in the market for products will affect the demand and price for those products. These considerations need to be taken into account when forecasting sales, and therefore costs of sales.

6.2 Market analysis

So a business has to consider not only product sales trends but also the stage of the life cycle of each product and the state of the market for that product.

However, the analysis could go even further, into the general state of the environment in which the business operates. This can often be efficiently done by carrying out a PEST analysis. This examines the following factors:

- **P**olitical
- **E**conomic
- **S**ocial
- **T**echnological

6.2.1 Political factors

Political factors may affect a forecast of future sales, and in turn, costs. This might particularly be the case if the business is an exporter, as the political development of other countries can either help or hinder the export drive.

In the UK, legislation such as health and safety, and minimum wage requirements might have an effect on the cost of producing products.

6.2.2 Economic factors

The general economic climate will have a huge effect on the sales of a business, and indeed, on its costs. All economies have stages, similar to the product life cycle. The four main stages are:

- **Recession** – Employment, consumer confidence and consumer spending start to fall.

- **Depression** – Heavy unemployment and low consumer demand are typical in this phase, though very often economies go straight from recession to recovery without experiencing depression.

- **Recovery** – Investment and employment start to regenerate and consumer spending rises.

- **Boom** – Consumer spending is rising fast.

Clearly, these factors will affect the future forecast for sales, and therefore costs of a business. For example, if the trend of sales has been taken from historical data collected in a recovery period followed by a boom period, and a period of recession is about to follow, then the projected trend figure will be completely misleading.

6.2.3 Social factors

The way in which society operates and changes can have a fundamental effect on the sales of a business, and therefore costs. Factors such as family sizes, lifestyle expectations, divorce rates and average life span can all affect, in the medium to long term, the prospects for sales of a particular product. Other factors such as fashion and health concerns can also impact upon the future sales of a business product.

6.2.4 Technological factors

Technological factors are probably one of the most important factors in the current high-tech consumer market place. Once a product is outdated and replaced by superior technology, then this will have a huge impact on sales levels.

For example, the launch of PlayStation 2 virtually ended sales of the original PlayStation; PS3 had the same effect on its predecessor.

Also the availability of faster machinery may make it difficult to use current output levels as a basis for forecasting future production output. (We will look at budget flexing in Chapter 7, which retrospectively amends a budget to be based on actual output.)

Technological advances can also change the nature of production. The advent of advanced manufacturing technology is changing the cost structure of many firms. Direct labour costs are reducing in significance, while fixed manufacturing costs are increasing. This causes forecasting difficulties because of the resulting changes in cost behaviour patterns.

Activity 11: External environment and costs

You have prepared a draft budget for direct material costs for a company which manufactures tables and chairs using wood from Scandinavian trees. You use two regular suppliers in Norway, but the Production Director is concerned about the impact of the external environment and other external specific costs.

Required

Write an email to the Production Director explaining the impact of external factors in the environment and any specific external costs that could affect the budget forecast.

Email

To: Production Director	**Date**: Exam
From: A Accountant	**Subject**: External Factors

7 Market research and sampling

Market research as a method of estimating demand for a product is particularly appropriate before the launch of a new product or substantially modified product. Market research will normally involve finding out the opinions of potential customers regarding the product and will always involve taking a sample of customers.

Sampling involves collecting data about a small number of items from the whole **population**, which is then used to estimate data regarding the whole population.

There are several methods of sampling:

7.1 Random sampling

Random sampling can be used when the entire population being considered is known. Random numbers are used to select a sample from the population.

When the sampling is completed and the results considered, then the sample results can be used to infer results for the whole population.

7.2 Stratified sampling

Stratified sampling is a type of random sampling which seeks to divide (or 'stratify') a population into groups, and then selects a random sample from each group based on the proportionate size of each group.

This is done by dividing the number in each group by the total population, and then multiplying this fraction by the overall sample.

Illustration 5: Stratified sampling

Company A has 75,000 customers in the north; 36,500 customers in the east; 90,000 customers in the south; and 98,500 customers in the west regions of the country.

The sample number of customers to be interviewed from each area of the country to obtain a representative response from 5,000 questionnaires is as follows.

Region	North	East	South	West	Total
Number of customers	75,000	36,500	90,000	98,500	300,000
Sample	1,250 (W1)	608 (W2)	1,500 (W3)	1,642 (W4)	5,000

Workings

(W1) (75,000/300,000) × 5,000 = 1,250

(W2) (36,500/300,000) × 5,000 = 608

(W3) (90,000/300,000) × 5,000 = 1,500

(W4) (98,500/300,000) × 5,000 = 1,642

7.3 Quota sampling

Quota sampling is used in situations where a number of different groups of the population can be identified. The number of samples required from each group is then determined and the data is taken from that required number in a non-random manner.

The main difference from stratified sampling is that with stratified sampling, individuals within each group are selected at random. With quota sampling, individuals are selected on a non-random basis.

For example, if a business has commissioned a market research survey about a potential major new product, it may decide that it wants public views of this product from the following relevant consumers:

• Males aged 18 to 30	200 samples
• Males aged 31 to 40	100 samples
• Females aged 18 to 30	300 samples
• Females aged 31 to 40	250 samples

The market researchers would then collect the information from individuals until each quota is satisfied on a totally non-random basis. This is the type of sampling that will often be used by researchers standing in the street, who question people that walk by.

7.4 Limitations of market research and sampling

Care must be taken in the market research to ensure that the sampling is as unbiased as possible, so that the results are representative of the sample as a whole.

A further problem with market research is that it can be expensive. Therefore, the cost and benefits of the research must be considered to determine if it should be carried out.

8 Uncertainties in forecasting

All forecasts are likely to include errors, but be aware of some of the following general limitations in the use of forecasting:

- The more data that is used, the better the results of the forecast will be, so a forecast based on limited data will inevitably be of limited use.

- The further into the future that the forecast considers, the more unreliable it will become.

- Forecast figures will often be based upon the assumption that current conditions will continue into the future, eg extrapolation of a trend based upon historical data, which may not be a valid assumption.

- If the forecast is based upon a trend, there are always random elements or variations which cause the trend to change.

- The forecast produced from the historical data may be quite accurate but the actual future results may be very different from the forecast figures due to changes in the political, economic or technological environment within which the business operates.

Uncertainties in forecasting can be addressed by using techniques such as planning models, regular reforecasting, rebudgeting, rolling budgets and budget flexing. We will look at rolling budgets in Chapter 3; and budget flexing in Chapter 7.

Assessment focus point

In assessments, the limitations of any income or expenditure forecasts will depend upon each scenario and the task set. Therefore, try to use the information given and consider these general limitations within that context.

Chapter summary

- The creation of budgets requires information or data.

- Both internal and external sources of data and information must be used in forecasting and budgeting.

- Internal data and information can be found from the historical financial accounting records, files of documents such as invoices, payroll details and inventory records, and many other sources in an organisation.

- External data and information can be found from government statistics, trade journals, newspapers and the internet.

- To prepare budgets, forecasts must be constructed.

- Forecasts of activity will be required, in particular for the key budget factor (limiting factor), but also for other elements of income and expense.

- The key budget factor may not necessarily be sales demand but may instead be related to a shortage of materials, a shortage of suitable labour or a lack of production capacity.

- The natural starting point for a sales forecast would be information from the sales experts within the business.

- Market research may be an appropriate method of forecasting sales for a new or substantially improved product.

- Time series analysis can be used to estimate the trend for future periods and then by applying seasonal variations, to find the forecast sales figures.

- The position of a product within its life cycle needs to be taken into account when forecasting future demand.

- When looking at forecasts, consideration should also be given to market conditions – political, economic, social and technological factors.

- Indexing can also be used to look at trends over time. Index numbers measure the change in value of a figure over time, by reference to its value at a fixed point.

Keywords

- **Base period:** the period for which the index is expressed as 100 and against which all other period figures are compared

- **Forecast:** an estimate of what may happen in the future based upon historical data and knowledge of future changes

- **Index number:** conversion of actual figures compared to a base year where the base year index is expressed as 100

- **Key budget factor:** the element or resource of the business that places limitations on the activities of the business

- **Moving average:** the calculation of an average figure for the results of consecutive periods of time

- **Population:** all of the items of data we are interested in for a particular data collecting purpose

- **Plan:** a deliberate commitment or intent

- **Promotion:** the various means by which firms draw attention to their products and services at various points in the product life cycle

- **Quota sampling:** the number of items required from each group is determined and then a non-random sample is taken to provide the required numbers

- **Random sampling:** all items in the population are known and are picked using random numbers

- **Resource budget:** budget set for each resource and activity of the business, eg production, labour usage, materials usage and so on

- **Retail Price Index:** a measure of the increase or decrease in general prices in the UK

- **Sales budget:** a short-term forecast for income (derived from expected number of sales multiplied by the expected selling price)

- **Sampling:** a method of finding out information about a population by only testing a sample of the items in the population

- **Seasonal variations:** the regular short-term pattern of increases or decreases in figures in a time series

- **Time series:** a series of income or expense figures recorded for a number of consecutive periods

- **Time series analysis:** a method of calculating the trend and other relevant figures from a time series

- **Trend:** the underlying movements of the time series over the period

- **Product life cycle:** the various stages of sales growth and profitability that most products will go through in their lives (development, introduction, growth, maturity and decline)

Activity answers

Activity 1: Sources of information

Information required	Source
Inflation	National Statistics Office
Sales demand	Market research
Competitor wage rates	Trade association
Employment data	National Statistics Office
Cost of finance	Bank
Share prices	Stock listing in financial press

Activity 2: Sources of information 2

Information required	Source
Population figures for areas in the UK	Office for National Statistics
VAT rates	HM Revenue & Customs website
Possible sales prices achievable in the market place	Trade journal

Activity 3: Contacts for information

Task	Contact
Forecasting the labour rate for next year	HR manager
Reviewing the budget	Budget committee
Forecasting the quantity of materials per unit for next year	Production manager
Preparing the advertising budget	Marketing director

Activity 4: Materials budget

The materials budget should be £ 500,000

520,000 / 1.04 = 500,000

Activity 5: The additive model – YSP Games Ltd

(a) The trend refers to the general direction in which a time series changes over time. This could be a steady increase, decrease or static level.

The seasonal variation is a predicted movement away from the trend for segments of the time series. These segments could be hours, days or months.

(b)

Month	Dec	Jan	Feb	Mar	Apr	May	Jun	Jul	Aug	Sept	Oct	Nov
Trend ('000)	250	255	260	265	270	275	280	285	290	295	300	305
SV ('000)	350	(200)	(210)	(150)	(130)	(100)	(60)	0	0	150	175	175
Actual volume of sales ('000)	600	55	50	115	140	175	220	285	290	445	475	480

(c) **Forecast sales volumes for August X8 to December X8**

The trend rises by 5 each month, therefore:

Month	Aug	Sept	Oct	Nov	Dec
Trend ('000)	350	355	360	365	370
SV ('000)	0	150	175	175	350
Forecast sales volume ('000)	350	505	535	540	720

Activity 6: The additive model 2

Quarter	Underlying trend (W1) £	Seasonal Variation £	Forecast £
1	106,000	−8,000	**98,000**
2	106,000	−1,000	**105,000**
3	106,000	−2,000	**104,000**
4	106,000	+11,000	**117,000**
Year	106,000	0	**424,000**

(W1) The sales for the year are forecast to increase by 6%

£400,000 × 1.06 = £424,000.

This equates to an underlying trend of £106,000 per quarter.

Activity 7: Index numbers 1

(a) Jan X8 = $\dfrac{26.20}{24.95} \times 100 = 105$

Feb X8 = $\dfrac{26.80}{24.95} \times 100 = 107.41$

Mar X8 = $\dfrac{26.90}{24.95} \times 100 = 107.82$

$$\text{Apr X8} = \frac{25.80}{24.95} \times 100 = 103.41$$

(b) $£24.95 \times \dfrac{108.26}{100} = £27.01$ per kg

(c) $\dfrac{£27.01 - £24.95}{£24.95} = 8.26\%$

Activity 8: Index numbers 2 – JB Ltd

(a)

Month	Jan	Feb	Mar	Apr	May	Jun
Underlying cost per kg (£)	180	210	240	270	300	330
Seasonal variation (£)	40	12	–18	–8	15	–4
Actual cost/forecast cost (£)	220	222	222	262	315	326

(b) Index $= \dfrac{£80}{£50} \times 100 = \boxed{160}$

The percentage increase during this period is $\boxed{60\%}$

$$\frac{80 - 50}{50} \times 100\% = 60\%$$

Activity 9: Index numbers 3 – Tees R Us

(a) June X7 $= \dfrac{4.95}{4.8} \times 100 = 103.125$

Nov X7 $= \dfrac{5.1}{4.8} \times 100 = 106.25$

(b) $£4.80 \times \dfrac{108.25}{100} = £5.196$ or $£5.20$

(c) $\dfrac{£5.20 - £4.80}{£4.80} = 8.33$ per kg

Or

$$\frac{£5.196 - £4.80}{£4.80} = 8.25\%$$

Activity 10: Forward contract – Ashby Ltd

(a)

September	= £800 × 122/107	£912.15
October	= £800 × 106/107	£792.52
November	= £800 × 125/107	£934.58

(b)

Total cost for the 3 months is:

			£
912.15 × 80	=		72,972.00
792.52 × 80	=		63,401.60
934.58 × 80	=		74,766.40
			211,140.00

Forward contract cost = £900 × 80 = £72,000 × 3 months = £216,000

The contract does not result in a lower price.

Activity 11: External environment and costs

Email

To: Production Director	**Date**: Exam
From: A Accountant	**Subject**: External Factors

There are several external factors which could affect the budget forecast. These are likely to be less predictable than those factors within the organisation's control and should be considered when the company's budgets are drafted. Failure to do so could leave the company with products that are not going to make a profit.

Factors which could affect the company include:

- Possibility of material price increases

- Rise in the price of oil, thereby increasing transportation costs

- Issues with quality – if there is not a consistent supply of good quality materials, production could be delayed. This could lead to customers being dissatisfied or shopping elsewhere.

- Fluctuations in exchange rates, affecting the price of the wood

- Impact of changes in the world economy, eg banking crisis, threat of bankruptcy in EU countries etc

Plus any other valid suggestions.

Test your learning

1   You are constructing a budget and wish to obtain the following information. **Who would you contact to find the information?**

Information required	Source	
Budgeted units of production per product		▼
Price of materials		▼
Sales brochure costs		▼
Mortgage interest on factory		▼

Picklist for line items:

Buyer
Finance director
Marketing director
Production planning manager

2   Given below are the production cost figures for a business for the last year.

	£
July	397,500
August	403,800
September	399,600
October	405,300
November	406,100
December	408,500
January	407,900
February	410,400
March	416,000
April	413,100
May	417,500
June	421,800

If constructing a budget for the forthcoming year, using this data, suggest a technique which might be used to forecast production costs.

3   **Describe three sources for collecting information for the production of sales forecasts and their limitations.**

4   The sales data for the last three years have been subject to a time series analysis and the trend has been estimated as an increase of 1.5% per quarter in unit sales. The unit sales for Quarter 4 of 20X1 were 175,000 units.

The time series analysis also shows the following seasonal variations:

Quarter 1   +15%

Quarter 2   −10%

Quarter 3   −30%

Quarter 4   +25%

The forecast sales units for each of the four quarters of 20X2 are:

Quarter 1	
Quarter 2	
Quarter 3	
Quarter 4	

5   The trend figures for sales in units for a business for the four quarters of 20X0 and the seasonal variations are estimated as follows:

	Trend unit sales	Seasonal variations
Quarter 1	210,000 units	−16%
Quarter 2	212,600 units	−25%
Quarter 3	215,400 units	+18%
Quarter 4	217,200 units	+23%

The forecast sales units for each of the quarters of 20X0 are:

Quarter 1	
Quarter 2	
Quarter 3	
Quarter 4	

6   **State the five stages of a product life cycle.**

7   **What factors would be considered in a PEST analysis?**

8   The production and sales levels for the next six months for a business are estimated as follows:

	Jan	Feb	Mar	Apr	May	Jun
Production – units	1,200	1,320	1,480	1,280	1,300	1,340
Sales – units	1,250	1,300	1,320	1,320	1,400	1,400

Variable production costs are currently £14.00 per unit and variable selling costs are £6.00 per unit. The price indices for the production costs and selling costs are currently 142.3 and 121.0 respectively.

The anticipated price indices for production and selling costs for the next six months are given below:

	Jan	Feb	Mar	Apr	May	Jun
Production costs index	144.3	145.0	145.6	148.6	149.2	150.0
Selling costs index	121.5	122.0	122.7	123.4	124.1	125.0

Complete the following:

	Jan	Feb	Mar	Apr	May	Jun
Forecast variable production costs £						
Forecast variable selling costs £						

Budgetary control systems

3

Learning outcomes

2.1	**Identify budgetary responsibilities and accountabilities**
	• Describe the role of the budget committee
	• Describe the duties and responsibilities of the budget accountant
	• Describe the budgetary accountabilities of senior managers in typical organisations (chief executive and heads of marketing, sales, production, purchasing, finance and human resources)
3.1	**Discuss how budgeting can promote effective, ethical and focused management**
	• Create an effective budgeting system, built on honesty and transparency
	• Use budget planning and control to motivate the management team
	• Use budget planning and control to create a cycle of continuous improvement
	• Co-ordinate budgets to achieve goal congruence
	• Recognise the behaviours that threaten effective budgetary control by creating budgetary slack, rivalry and suboptimal performance
	• Discuss the benefits and risks of linking remuneration to budget achievement
3.2	**Discuss the use of budgeting for planning, coordinating, authorising and cost control**
	• How budgeting fulfils the four apparently diverse functions of planning, coordinating, authorising and cost control
	• Why a balance must be maintained (for example, overemphasis on cost control is likely to constrain business growth and high level planning targets can conflict with detailed coordination activity)
	• The potential for conflict between these functions
3.3	**Break a budget down into control periods**
	• Split the elements of an operating statement budget into appropriate time periods to facilitate regular reporting
	• Ensure that the planning assumptions and cost behaviours in the budget are correctly reflected in the split into control periods

4.1	**Discuss the basic methods of budgeting and make recommendations for their use**
	• The features of the basic methods:
	– Incremental (historical)
	– Zero based
	– Priority based
	– Activity based
	• The comparative advantages of each method
	• The circumstances in which each method should be recommended

Assessment context

It is important to understand the uses of budgetary control and to be prepared to break budgets down into, for example, monthly or weekly periods.

Qualification context

Budgetary control is only tested in this course.

Business context

A core part of any business is to determine its objectives and come up with a plan of how they will achieve these objectives (strategy). Budgeting provides detail of how the business should operate in order to achieve its objectives

Chapter overview

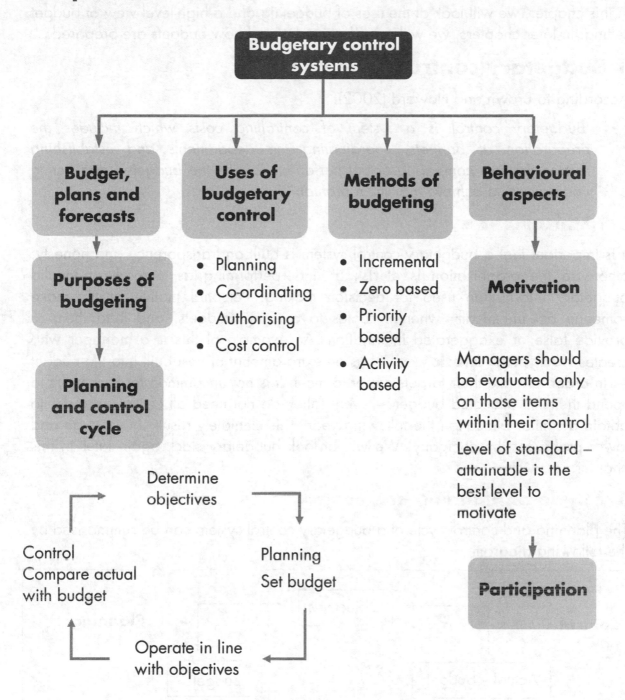

Budgetary control systems

Budget, plans and forecasts

Uses of budgetary control
- Planning
- Co-ordinating
- Authorising
- Cost control

Methods of budgeting
- Incremental
- Zero based
- Priority based
- Activity based

Behavioural aspects

Purposes of budgeting

Motivation

Managers should be evaluated only on those items within their control

Level of standard – attainable is the best level to motivate

Planning and control cycle

Determine objectives

Control
Compare actual with budget

Planning
Set budget

Operate in line with objectives

Participation

Introduction

In this chapter, we will look at the uses of budgeting and a high-level view of budget setting. In later chapters, we will consider the detail of how budgets are prepared.

1 Budgetary control systems

According to Brown and Howard (2002):

> 'Budgetary control is a system of controlling costs which includes the preparation of budgets, coordinating the departments and establishing responsibilities, comparing actual performance with the budgeted and acting upon results to achieve maximum profitability.'

1.1 Ethical issues

It is important that a budgetary control system is built on transparency and honesty; otherwise the organisation is at risk of underperforming as a result of invalid budgetary information used for decision making. Personal motives might make someone act unethically when it comes to creating budgets, and lead them to provide false or exaggerated information. An example of this is a manager who creates **budgetary slack** — which is an extra amount of cost built into the budget — in order to make their targets easier to meet. It is not uncommon for managers to spend their full allocated budget — even if they do not need all of it — in order to obtain a similar allocation the following year. This ultimately results in wastage and lower profits for the company. We will at look budgetary slack again later in this chapter.

1.2 Cycle of planning and control

The planning and control cycle of a budgetary control system can be summarised by the following diagram.

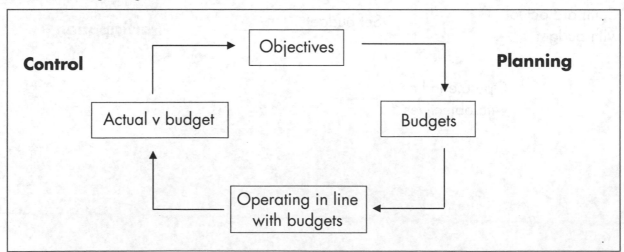

This diagram shows that the strategic objectives of a firm drive the budgets that are set. The company aims to operate within these budgets. This is measured by comparison of actual and budgeted results. Action can then be taken to improve performance, and this can feed back into the strategic objectives. This creates a cycle of continuous improvement in the organisation.

1.3 Uses of budgetary control

It is important that budgetary control fulfils and maintains the balance between four key areas:

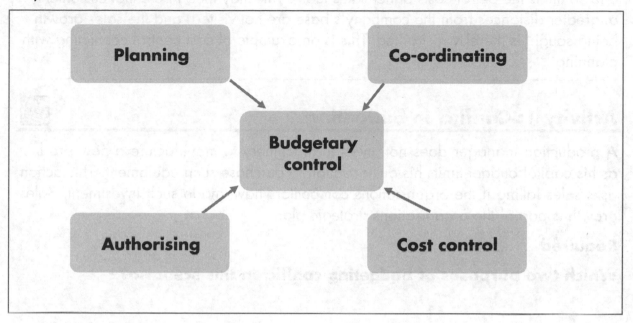

1.3.1 Planning

Budgeting forces management to look ahead, to set out detailed plans for achieving the targets for each department, operation and each manager.

1.3.2 Co-ordination

The activities of different departments need to be coordinated to ensure everyone in an organisation is working towards the same goals. This means, for example, that the purchasing department should base its budget on production requirements and that the production budget should, in turn, be based on sales expectations.

1.3.3 Authorisation

Expenditure must be authorised by the responsible budget manager.

1.3.4 Cost control

Existence of a budget will ensure managers try to limit the expenditure to that contained within the budget. Control over actual performance is provided by the comparisons of actual results against the budget plan. Departures from budget can then be investigated and the reasons for any departures can be divided into controllable and uncontrollable factors; and action taken to improve performance.

1.3.5 Potential for conflict

Emphasis on any one of these areas can damage the business elsewhere, so care needs to be taken to ensure that a balance between them is maintained.

For example, over-emphasis on cost control could prevent business growth as new opportunities are not authorised because they are not in the original budget.

Illustration 1: Conflict in budgeting

A sales director may be concerned about controlling the costs within her budget, and so limits the petrol costs of her sales team. This may mean potential customers at greater distances from the company's base are not visited, and the sales growth being sought is thereby restrained. This is an example of cost control conflicting with planning.

Activity 1: Conflict in budgeting

A production manager does not invest in machinery to manufacture a new product as his capital budget limits his authorisation to purchase such equipment. This action risks sales falling if the organisations competitors have made such investment. Sales growth is part of the organisations strategic plan.

Required

Which two purposes of budgeting conflict in this scenario?

2 Co-ordination of the setting of budgets

There are many functional budgets that need to be set and many of these are inter-related. Operational planning and budget-setting all takes place over a considerable period of time and often requires the involvement of many managers and staff of all levels. Therefore, it is important that budget setting is co-ordinated if any meaningful budgets are to be produced.

2.1 Budget committee

Many organisations will also have a **budget committee**, made up of senior executives, including the Chief Executive Officer, who are responsible for co-ordinating and administering all of the individual budgets, and who will review and authorise each individual budget. Each function of the business should be represented on the budget committee in order to ensure that there is full communication between all areas of the business.

Responsibility for individual budgets for different functions within the organisation lies with **budget holders**. A budget holder is a member of staff who has been assigned a budget for a particular function and is accountable to their senior manager for it.

The budget committee will normally be assisted by an accountant known as the budget officer, or **budget accountant**. They serve as the key link between the budget committee and the budget holders in preparing the budgets and ensuring budgetary control.

2.2 Budget accountant

The main role of a budget accountant is to assist in preparing the budget of an organisation, and ensure that it operates within this budget. To achieve this, their key duties are:

- **Preparing the budget for the organisation** – this involves liaising with the budget committee and budget holders to come up with a detailed budget of the costs and revenues for the organisation, typically for the coming year.

- **Preparing management accounts** – a typical monthly management accounts 'pack' compares actual statements of profit or loss to the budget and provides reasons for significant variances. These reports are compiled from the organisational accounting system, and reasons for variances are usually obtained from the budget holders.

- **Communicating results to senior management** – the budget accountant usually presents the management accounts to senior management, providing explanations for significant variances. They may also make recommendations for action for senior management to take, if this is necessary.

2.3 Budget manual

Many organisations will produce a **budget manual**, which is a set of instructions detailing how the budget is to be prepared. The budget manual might typically include the following:

- The names of the budget holders – those responsible for producing each budget
- The manager to whom each budget holder reports
- An organisational chart
- The timescale for the production of each budget
- The procedures for preparing each budget
- The format of the budgets
- How and when actual performance is compared to budget

2.4 Budget holders

As discussed above, a budget holder is a member of staff who has been assigned a budget for a particular activity. The budget holder will prepare the budget for their function, with the assistance of the budget accountant.

In a typical organisation, the budget holder is the manager who will also be responsible for ensuring that the activities of their department meet the budget. For example:

Manager	Budget responsibility
Head of Sales	Sales
Head of Marketing	Marketing
Head of Production	Production
Head of Purchasing	Materials purchasing

In addition, other departments play a crucial role in providing critical information for the budget. For example, the head of Human Resources can provide information such as salaries, pension costs and national insurance costs, to formulate the direct and indirect labour budgets.

Once the budget holder has drafted their budget, they will then submit this to the budget committee. The budget accountant will ensure that the budget is consistent with other resource budgets, checking, for example, that the purchasing budget has been prepared in line with the production budget.

There will then frequently be negotiations between the budget committee and the budget holder regarding the detailed content of the budget. The manager might, for example, have built in an increase in costs over previous years which the budget committee does not agree with. The budget holder may well have to change their draft budget and re-submit it to the budget committee a number of times before the budget committee is satisfied with it.

2.5 Master budget

Once the budget committee has agreed all of the resource budgets with the budget holders, they will then be incorporated into the **master budget**, which normally takes the form of a budgeted statement of profit or loss, budgeted statement of financial position and a cash budget.

Activity 2: Budget committee

Required

Who should sit on the budget committee?

2.6 Rolling budgets

A **rolling budget** is a budget that is continually updated by adding the next accounting period when the current accounting period is over.

A budget is set on a quarterly basis for the next year. The January to March budget is set out in detail while the budget for the period from April to December is usually less detailed. At the end of March, the detailed budget is created for April to June, along with an additional outline budget for the quarter from January to March of the following year, which is added in later.

This has the advantage of giving budget holders and the budget committee an opportunity to react to changes in circumstances; however, it also means that budgeting will tend to be done more frequently and take up more management time.

The breakdown of budgets themselves into control periods is discussed further in this chapter.

3 Motivation

We discussed earlier that a budget is used to monitor and evaluate performance, by comparing budgeted and actual performance, in order to drive improved performance across an organisation. Given that managers and their staff are judged on this comparison — that is, they are accountable for the actual performance compared with budgets — budgets can be used as a tool to motivate.

For the budgetary control system to be at its most effective, employees and managers must be motivated to ensure that the budget is met. However, as we will see below, budgetary controls systems can also produce certain undesirable behaviours — for example, budgetary slack, rivalry and sub-optimal performance.

As we mentioned earlier, there are ethical issues involved in creating budgets. Sometimes the personal motives of staff can conflict with creating a budget that is honest and transparent. The key areas that a business should consider when setting up the budgetary system are:

- Who sets the budgets – participation
- How achievable the budgets are
- Goal congruence
- Performance related pay

3.1 Motivation vs control

It is important to distinguish between measures of performance for individual managers and the measures of performance of what it is that they manage.

It is necessary to consider a manager's performance based only upon those items that are directly controllable by that manager.

3.2 Top down budgeting

Top down budgeting is a method of setting budgets whereby senior management are made solely responsible for the setting of the budgets, and these are then imposed upon lower level managers, who are in turn responsible for meeting these targets.

The advantages of this are:

- Senior management will incorporate the strategic plans into all of the budgets.

- The resource (or cost) budgets will all be in harmony with each other.

- Senior management has an overview of all of the resources of the business.

- The budget should be produced more quickly.

- Input from junior management, who may not have the skills or knowledge necessary for the budgeting process, is eliminated.

The disadvantages are:

- Managers may become demotivated by the prospect of working to meet targets that someone else has set.

- The managers' detailed knowledge of a particular resource is ignored.

- The initiative of lower level management may be stifled.

- Managers may resent other departments for being allocated a proportionally greater share of the budget of the organisation, leading to rivalry between departments.

- Rivalry could also arise between departments, if they blame each other for not meeting their targets.

3.3 Bottom up budgeting

In **bottom up budgeting**, budgets are prepared by functional managers based upon their detailed knowledge of a particular resource and the costs associated with it. In practice, these budgets are then normally reviewed by the budget committee and a process of negotiation then takes place in which the requirements of senior management are balanced against what managers believe is possible.

The advantages of this method are:

- Budgets are based on the detailed working knowledge of managers.

- The motivation of the managers to achieve a budget which they have set should be increased.

- The managers' commitment to the strategic plans of the company should be increased.

There are disadvantages though:

- The outcome of negotiations with the budget committee may cause dissatisfaction.

- The budgeting process will take more time and involve more personnel.

- There may be a lack of co-ordination between resource budgets that must be corrected.

- Managers may be tempted to introduce budgetary slack in order to ensure that when the actual results are compared to the budget, the outcome is favourable.

3.4 Budgetary slack

Budgetary slack is the difference between the minimum necessary costs and those costs built into the budget or which are actually incurred.

In the process of preparing budgets, managers might **deliberately overestimate costs and underestimate sales**, so that they will not be blamed in the future for overspending and poor results.

In controlling actual operations, managers must then **ensure that their spending rises to meet their budget**; otherwise they will be 'blamed' for careless budgeting.

A typical situation is where a manager **pads the budget** and wastes money on non-essential expenses so that they use up all of their budgetary allowances. The reason behind their action is a fear that unless the allowance is fully spent, it will be reduced in future periods, thus making their job more difficult, as the future reduced budgets will not be so easy to attain.

When inefficiency and slack are allowed for in budgets, achieving a budget target will only mean that costs have remained within accepted levels of inefficient spending.

Activity 3: Budgetary slack

A designer at a small website design company has been asked by the managing director to prepare a budget for the coming quarter. It usually takes him, or his staff, about two days to design a website; but in the budget, he allows for 2.5 days per new website.

Required

What problems might this lead to when assessing the performance of the design department?

3.5 Attainable budgets and sub-optimal performance

Budgets can be set in an ideal manner or in an attainable manner.

If a budget is seen as ideal and therefore impossible to achieve, this can have a de-motivating effect. The manager and employees will perceive the budget as 'ridiculous' and not even attempt to achieve it, leading to sub-optimal performance. However, if a budget is set at a level which is challenging but essentially attainable, then this can be motivating to the manager and the employees, who will set about trying to meet the budget figures.

3.6 Negotiated budgeting

In practice, the different levels of management often agree budgets by a process of negotiation.

Final budgets are therefore most likely to lie between what top management would really like and what junior managers believe is feasible.

3.7 Goal congruence

The aim of the budget should be to move the business further towards its strategic goals. If the managers of a business are personally motivated to meet their budgets and therefore, to move towards the strategic goal, then there is said to be **goal congruence** within the business.

Goal congruence amongst employees, managers and senior management is not easy to achieve within a business, particularly as the question of motivation of managers and employees is very dependent on the personalities of the individuals involved.

However, it is possible to try to achieve goal congruence, particularly if the employees' and managers' remuneration packages are set in such a way that the employee or manager is better off financially if they do work towards a corporate goal.

3.8 Performance related pay

Performance related pay is a method of remunerating employees or managers in such a way that their total remuneration increases if they meet organisational goals and targets. This may take the form of bonuses or share options or other incentives.

In order for any form of performance related pay to be successful in motivating managers to meet budgetary targets, the following elements must be in place:

- Managers must know the strategic goals of the business and must be able to see how their budgets work towards this strategic goal.

- The managers' budgets must be achievable, although challenging.

- The managers must have control over the costs that are being compared to the budget and must feel that they have the ability and freedom to meet the budgetary targets; a manager must not feel that their performance is dependent upon that of others.

- The rewards being offered by the business must be great enough to have an effect.

Performance related bonuses tend only to work when there is a short timescale between the target being met and the reward being received. This can, however, lead to a concentration by managers on meeting short-term goals, rather than looking at the long-term aims of the business. As with all efforts directed at motivation, the success of performance related pay will depend largely on the individual's attitude to work in general; and to the bonus system, in particular.

Activity 4: Performance related pay

An accountancy firm operates a bonus scheme for its managers. Individual managers and departments are set fee targets in the budget at the start of the year. The terms of the bonus scheme are such that Sally, a tax manager, will receive her bonus if she meets her individual targets and if the tax department meets its targets.

Required

Write an email to the Managing Partner, describing the benefits and problems of using these budget targets to determine the bonus scheme.

4 Control periods within a budget

It is usual for an organisation to complete a budget which covers a full year. However, depending on the needs of the organisation, the budget will also be broken down into smaller time periods or control periods such as quarters, months, weeks or even days.

Such a breakdown is required because the comparison of the budgeted figures and the actual performance achieved by a business is used by management to monitor and control. What they find out from this evaluation may lead them to take decisions which may alter their initial plans. Suitable time intervals for making such decisions may correspond to the pattern by which a business generates income and incurs costs.

It is important that the behaviour of costs is correctly reflected in the split of control periods. If a particular cost is likely to vary from month to month, it would not be accurate to split the annual budgeted cost evenly by twelve months.

More information is required to establish the expected distribution of spending over the year. When budgets are prepared, the budget accountant and budget holders need to identify the key planning assumptions that will affect how costs are spread over the year.

For example, the marketing department of a company might have large marketing campaigns planned for the months of March, June, September and December. It is therefore reasonable to assume that spending in, say, printed material will peak during these months, and therefore this cost behaviour needs to be reflected in the control periods.

Illustration 2: Control periods

A **manufacturing business** may have a budget split into weekly targets. If the monitoring of performance shows that there was idle time above that budgeted for (that is, the available time of labour that week exceeded the actual hours required), the production department may take the decision to increase production and store any product not yet required, or redeploy workers to other areas of the business.

Other decisions may surround price. If the sales volume of a product is lower than budgeted, a decision may be taken to discount the price of the product to boost sales and shift inventory. Such monitoring and the resulting actions need to be taken on a timely basis. If the manager responsible were to wait until the end of the year to look at such issues, it would be too late to take the appropriate action to counter it.

A **solicitor's firm** may have an annual budget broken down into months. It will pay its staff salaries on a monthly basis and may also bill clients monthly. This means the actual results of the business are determined on a monthly basis and so it is appropriate that the budget reflects the same time periods, in order for any meaningful comparison to be made.

A **chain of bars** may have a budget broken into weekly periods. This is because levels of activity in the bars may vary significantly from week to week if, for example, during some weeks important football matches are played which attract people to the bars, and so increased sales figures are forecast then.

A major **chain of department stores** may have a daily budget for sales generated during a sale period, to make decisions regarding further price changes which may be required on a daily basis.

Activity 5: Control periods

A community social club holds a quarterly family fun day to raise funds for its activities throughout that quarter.

Required

What control periods should the club prepare its budgets for?

5 Methods of budgeting

In Chapter 4, we will look more closely at the details of setting up each of the budget types, but in this chapter, we will consider the overall methods that might be adopted to set the resource (ie cost) budgets for each period.

> **Assessment focus point**
>
> You will not be asked simply to list the advantages and disadvantages of a particular method, although you do need to know them. You need to be able to identify the method being used in a particular scenario, and know and understand whether it is appropriate or not.
>
> A task may present you with a budget prepared using one method (without necessarily naming the method used, but describing how the budget has been constructed). You may be asked to assess the suitability of the method applied, and suggest an alternative.

5.1 Incremental budgeting

One of the most common methods of setting the budget for a period is **incremental budgeting**. Under this method, the budget for the forthcoming period is set by taking the budget for the previous period and adding on a percentage to reflect any increases in prices or changes in activity level since the last budget was set.

Incremental budgeting would be appropriate for those businesses whose costs are not expected to change significantly.

The advantages of incremental budgeting are:

- It is a fairly simple procedure that will not require too much management time.

- The budget is stable and changes are only gradual.

- Co-ordination of budgets is made easier.

However the disadvantages are:

- Any inefficiencies in the original budget are repeated each period.

- There is no incentive to reduce costs or develop new ideas.

- The budgets may become out of date.

- There may be budgetary slack built into the budget, meaning that meeting the budget is easier for managers as this slack remains each year.

Illustration 3: Incremental budgeting

The Rugby Club's advertising budget last year was £100,000. This year, it is anticipated that 20% more advertising will be made and that inflation has been 2%.

The advertising budget for this year would be: £100,000 x 20% = £120,000 – for the additional advertising

£120,000 x 1.02 = £122,400 – for inflation

5.2 Zero based budgeting (ZBB)

Zero based budgeting, as the name implies, is a method of budgeting whereby the budget for each cost centre is looked at from scratch for each period.

The main point about zero based budgeting is that every item of expenditure must be justified before it can be included in the budget. This will often be approached from an activity-based perspective on the basis that, in general, it is activities that incur costs.

For each item of activity that leads to an expense, a decision package is compiled in which the following questions must be asked and answered:

- Is the activity necessary?
- Are there alternatives to this activity (eg outsourcing)?
- What are the costs of the alternative?
- What would happen if the activity were not carried out?
- Is the expense of the activity worth the benefit?

By asking such questions, the activity and its related expenditure can be justified for inclusion in the budget; or a cheaper alternative found.

ZBB is not particularly useful for production departments where costs are largely dependent upon the levels of production and sales. However, it can be a useful technique for service department costs such as the maintenance or personnel departments. It can also be a useful method for factoring in discretionary costs such as advertising and training.

The advantages of zero based budgeting are:

- It challenges the *status quo* and forces an organisation to examine alternative activities and existing expenditure levels.

- Any inefficiencies in the budget in one period are not automatically reproduced in the budget for the next period.

- Inefficient practices can be removed.

- The cost effectiveness of work practices and procedures is constantly being monitored.

- Budgetary slack should be eliminated.

The disadvantages of the method are:

- It is time consuming, complex and costly.
- Short-term benefits are emphasised which may be detrimental in the long term.

5.3 Programme based budgeting

Programme based budgeting is a method of budgeting that is suitable for non-profit making organisations. It is a method whereby the work of the organisation is split into programmes which are designed to achieve the organisational objectives.

Different departments of the organisation may be involved in more than one programme but the funds for the business are allocated to the programmes rather than to the departments.

As there will usually not be enough funds to achieve all of the programmes, decisions must be made as to which programmes will be supported and at what level.

5.4 Activity based budgeting

Activity based budgeting (ABB) is a system of setting budgets based upon activity based costing principles, which were considered in Chapter 1. The principle of both activity based costing and budgeting is that the costs of activities are caused (driven) by the cost drivers. For example, the costs of the works canteen will (largely) be driven by the number of meals served. When budgeting on this basis the numbers of each cost driver that will be incurred must be considered and the cost of that cost driver.

The advantages of activity based budgeting include:

- It attempts to provide meaningful product costs.
- It recognises that many overhead costs arise out of the diversity and complexity of operations.
- It facilitates a good understanding of what drives overhead costs, so they can be better managed.

The disadvantages of activity based budgeting include:

- Time involved in identifying activities and drivers may be significant.
- The ability of a single cost driver to explain fully the cost behaviour of all items in its associated pool, is questionable.
- Some costs may not be able to relate to production output eg the cost of the annual external audit.

5.5 Priority based budgeting

Priority-based budgeting is a similar method of budgeting to zero-based budgeting, and is often used in public sector organisations. Priority based budgeting, however, does not start from a zero base. Activities are re-evaluated when budgets are set. Like zero-based budgeting, decision packages are compiled for each activity. Resources are then allocated to decision packages based on the level of priority.

Activity 6: Methods of budgeting

A charity carries out different projects each year, raising funds specifically to cover the costs of those projects. The finance officer is preparing the budget for the coming year by increasing all costs of the prior year to reflect current inflation.

Required

Write an email to the finance officer, explaining why this method of budgeting may not be appropriate for the charity, and suggest a suitable alternative.

Email

To: Finance Officer	**Date**: 01/04/20XX
From: A Accountant	**Subject**: Methods of budgeting

Chapter summary

- Budgets can help management in their planning and control functions, in authorising and co-ordinating departments and functions, and in motivating employees.

- The budget manual and budget committee are usually essential elements of control within the budgeting process.

- There are various ways of implementing a budgetary control system, each of which is likely to have behavioural effects on management. These include top down and bottom up budgeting, and negotiated budgeting.

- If the managers of the business are personally motivated to work towards the same goals as the business, then there is said to be goal congruence – one method of achieving goal congruence is through a system of performance related pay.

- Budgets are broken down into smaller control periods to enable monitoring of performance and subsequent actions to take place on a timely basis. The intervals of the budget may correspond to the income and expenditure pattern of the organisation.

BPP
LEARNING MEDIA

Keywords

- **Bottom up budgeting:** a budgeting system in which operational managers have a degree of input into the budget

- **Budget:** a formalised, numerical, often financial, plan of action

- **Budget accountant:** an accountant who helps the budget committee in the preparation of budgets

- **Budget committee:** committee of senior executives from all areas of the business who oversee the preparation of the budgets

- **Budget holder:** the manager responsible for preparing a resource budget

- **Budget manual:** set of detailed instructions as to how the budget should be prepared

- **Budgetary slack:** an extra amount of cost built into a budget by managers in order to make targets easier to meet

- **Goal congruence:** the aims of the individual functions or departments are consistent with the aims of the organisation overall

- **Master budget:** budgeted statement of profit or loss, budgeted statement of financial position and cash budget

- **Negotiated budgeting:** a budgeting system in which operational managers and senior management negotiate the final budget

- **Performance related pay:** method of remuneration which rewards managers or employees for reaching set targets

- **Plan:** a deliberate commitment or intent

- **Rolling budget:** a budget that is constantly updated to cover the next 12 month period

- **Top down budgeting:** a budgeting system in which the budget is set and imposed by senior management

Activity 1: Conflict in budgeting

Authorisation and planning

Activity 2: Budget committee

The budget committee should be made up of senior executives from all functional areas of the business, plus the budget officer.

Activity 3: Budgetary slack

The company is using bottom up budgeting in order to create the budget. This might motivate the design team to work hard to achieve the budget because they feel part of the budgeting process, and believe that the targets set are realistic. However, the designer has built in budgetary slack in order to make the budget easier to meet. This will often have the outcome of causing favourable variances when actual costs are compared to the budget, even if there is no real improvement in performance.

Activity 4: Performance related pay

Email

To: Managing Partner	**Date**: 01/04/20XX
From: A Accountant	**Subject**: Bonus scheme

The benefits are that all the managers of a department are motivated to achieve the firm's goals. It is of benefit to all managers if the workload is spread amongst them. However, even if Sally works hard and achieves the targets set for her, she cannot receive her bonus if her colleagues do not work as hard. This can be de-motivating.

As the fee targets are set at the start of the year and not reviewed, the scheme could have a further de-motivating effect — for example, if staff leave and are not replaced but the departmental target does not take account of fewer available chargeable hours (which can be converted into fees).

The staff who are not managers have no incentive to work hard, as they cannot participate in the scheme.

Activity 5: Control periods

As income is received and then spent on a quarterly basis, a suitable period for the budget to cover is a quarter. In reality, an annual budget may be drawn up, which is then split into quarters.

Activity 6: Methods of Budgeting

Email

To: Finance Officer	**Date**: 01/04/20XX
From: A Accountant	**Subject**: Methods of budgeting

The method of budgeting you are using is an incremental method of budgeting that simply increases the costs of the previous year. This is inappropriate, as the activities of the charity change from year to year, so the actual resources that have to be bought, including labour costs, or services which must be paid for, will vary significantly from the prior year.

It is not just the cost of these that will vary because of inflation, but the charity's use of these resources. A more suitable alternative would be to use programme based budgeting. This would look at each of the projects being funded, and in turn, consider the resource requirement, and then build a budget accordingly.

1   **Explain what is meant by a budget and how budgets can be useful.**

2   **In a bottom up budgeting system, with a full budget committee, explain how the budget for the next 12 months would be set.**

3   **Select the appropriate person to contact in each of the following situations:**

The draft budget is ready for review: ▼

The managing director needs help in interpreting the draft budget: ▼

Picklist:

The budget accountant
The budget committee
The budget holder

4   **Explain how far performance related pay may help in ensuring goal congruence between managers and the organisation.**

Budget preparation

4

Learning outcomes

2.3	**Prepare planning schedules for physical production resources** • Production plan (volumes of inventory, production and sales) • Material usage and purchases • Staffing, labour hours and overtime • Plant utilisation
2.5	**Prepare draft budgets from historical data, forecasts and planning assumptions** • Sales revenue • Material usage and purchases • Labour (employees and other resources) • Production facilities • Other overheads • Operating statement (profit and loss account down to operating profit) • Capital expenditure
3.5	**Integrate standard costing into budgetary control** • Incorporate standard costs into budget calculations • Explain how the use of standard costing can complement budgetary control
4.2	**Plan and agree draft budgets with all parties involved** • Describe the sources of Information and the validity of those sources when submitting draft budgets to management • Identify the key planning assumptions in a prepared budget • Identify the potential threats to budget achievement • Identify the responsibilities of relevant managers • Quantify the impact of the budget on the organisation • Submit the budget for approval

Assessment context

Preparation of budgets will be examined via many of the tasks in the exam.

Qualification context

Budget preparation is only tested in this course.

Business context

A core part of any business is to determine its objectives and come up with a plan of how they will achieve these objectives (strategy). Budgeting provides detail of how the business should operate in order to achieve its objectives.

Chapter overview

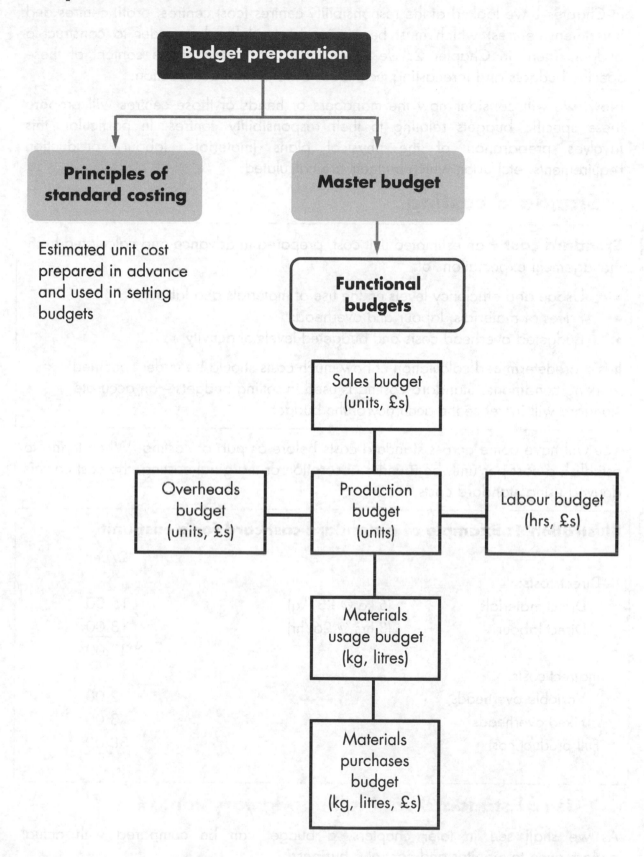

Introduction

In Chapter 1 we looked at the responsibility centres (cost centres, profit centres and investment centres) which must be appropriately defined in order to construct a budget. Then, in Chapter 2, we looked in closer detail at the content of these specific budgets and forecasting techniques used in their construction.

Now, we will consider how the managers or heads of those centres will prepare these specific budgets relating to their responsibility centres. In particular, this involves preparation of the physical plans (materials, labour, production requirements, etc) upon which budgets are calculated.

1 Standard costing

Key term

Standard cost – an estimated unit cost, prepared in advance and calculated from management expectations of:

- Usage and efficiency levels on the use of materials and labour
- Prices of materials, labour and overheads
- Budgeted overhead costs and budgeted levels of activity.

It is a predetermined calculation of how much costs should be under specified working conditions. Standard costing is used in setting budgets – an accurate standard will increase the accuracy of the budget.

You will have come across standard costs before as part of costing. When trying to establish a cost per unit, be it under absorption or marginal costing, the cost card is derived using standard costs.

Illustration 1: Example of a standard cost card for a cost unit

		£/unit
Direct costs:		
Direct materials	(5 kg @ £3/kg)	15.00
Direct labour	(3 hrs @ £6/hr)	18.00
		33.00
Indirect costs:		
Variable overheads		2.00
Fixed overheads		3.00
Full product cost		38.00

1.1 Use of standard costing in budgetary control

As we shall see in later chapters, a budget can be compared with actual performance to monitor and control a business.

Broken down, on a line by line basis, this effectively compares standard costs with actual costs. This comparison leads to the calculation of differences (variances). Variances are discussed in Chapter 7.

These are investigated by management, and actions can then be taken to rectify any performance issues. The action may lead to the setting of new standards, and so there is a cycle of continuous improvement.

The purposes of a budget in planning and control are therefore facilitated by standard costing but here we look at constructing budgets using standard costs.

1.2 Types of standard

There are a number of different approaches that can be used when determining standard cost.

1.2.1 Ideal standards

Ideal standards are standard costs which are set on the basis that ideal working conditions apply. Therefore, there is no allowance for wastage, inefficiencies or idle time when setting the materials and labour cost standards.

There are two main problems with using ideal standards in budgeting:

Planning – if ideal standards are used for planning purposes, it is likely that the results will be inaccurate, as the standard does not reflect the reality of working conditions. Therefore, if a labour cost standard is set with no allowance for any inefficiency or idle time in operations, the reality is that the operations will take longer or will require more employees than planned for.

Control – if ideal standards are compared to actual costs, then this will usually result in adverse variances, as the reality is that there will always be some inefficiencies and wastage. This can de-motivate managers and employees who will feel that, in reality, these standards can never be met and therefore, they may stop trying to meet them. A further problem with these adverse variances is that they will be viewed as the norm and be ignored, meaning that any corrective action that might be required is not taken.

1.2.2 Attainable standards

Attainable standards are ones that better reflect the reality of the workplace and which allow for small amounts of normal wastage and inefficiency. An attainable standard is one that is achievable; however, it will only be met if operations are carried out efficiently and cost-effectively.

If attainable standards are well set, then the variances that result will tend to be a mixture of favourable and adverse variances, as sometimes the standard will be exceeded and sometimes it will not quite be met. Attainable standards are often viewed as motivational to managers and employees as they are not out of reach in the way that ideal standards are, but they can be met if all goes to plan.

1.2.3 Basic standards

Basic standards are the historical standard costs, probably the ones set when the product was first produced. As such, they are likely to be out of date, as they will not have taken account of inflation or any changes in working practices.

If basic standards are used to compare to actual costs, then this will tend to result in large variances, both adverse and favourable, depending upon how out of date the basic standard is. These variances will therefore be little more than meaningless. For this reason, basic standards are rarely used for variance analysis but may still be kept as historical information alongside other, more up-to-date standards.

Activity 1: Ideal standards

A production manager is preparing a budget using a materials standard cost which makes no allowance for materials wastage in the production process. The manager says that this encourages workers to be careful with their use of material. The most experienced workers produce wastage of around 2% of the material they use.

Explain the problem with the use of this materials standard cost and suggest how the production manager should set the standard.

2 Preparing sales and resource budgets

The process of preparing sales and resource budgets involves:

- Determining the **key budget factor**, as discussed in Chapter 2. For the purposes of this chapter, it is assumed that the key budget factor is sales, and this determines the sales forecast

    - The resource budgets (ie production, materials usage, materials purchase, labour usage, labour cost, machine hours, variable and fixed overheads budgets) then flow from the sales forecast.

    - Preparing the 'physical' plans in the case of each production resource which fit with sales forecasts eg determining quantities of material required, labour hours or machine hours necessary.

- Taking these physical plans and creating financial plans ie converting the physical quantities into costs, using standard costs; this gives specific resource budgets.
- Combining all resource budgets, and sales (income) budgets, along with capital and cash budgets to create a master budget for the organisation.

2.1 Sales budget

Forecasting the quantity of sales for future periods was considered in Chapter 2. Once the expected quantity of sales has been determined, then the anticipated price to be charged for the products or services can be applied to this forecast. This gives us the budgeted income, usually referred to as the **sales revenue budget** (in £). From the sales budget, the resource budgets for production can also be prepared.

Illustration 2: Sales budget

Oliver Engineering produces a single product, the Stephenson. For budgeting purposes, the year is divided into 13 four week periods, with five working days each week and therefore 20 working days per period. The forecast sales quantities for the first five periods of 20X0 are as follows:

Units				
Period 1	**Period 2**	**Period 3**	**Period 4**	**Period 5**
10,000	12,000	15,000	13,000	11,000

The current selling price of the Stephenson is £40, although it is anticipated that there will be a 10% price increase in Period 4.

The sales revenue budget can now be prepared.

	Forecast revenue £
Period 1 (10,000 × £40)	400,000
Period 2 (12,000 × £40)	480,000
Period 3 (15,000 × £40)	600,000
Period 4 (13,000 × £44)	572,000
Period 5 (11,000 × £44)	484,000
	2,536,000

3 Production budget

Once the sales budget has been prepared, the next stage is to prepare the **production budget** in finished goods units. There are two factors that will affect the amount of production required:

- Any changes in inventory levels of finished goods that are anticipated
- The level of defective finished goods that are forecast

3.1 Changes in finished goods inventory levels

If all goods produced can be sold, and there is to be no change in the levels of finished goods held in inventory, then the amount that must be produced is the same as the quantity of forecast sales.

However, if the level of finished goods held in inventory is to change, then this will affect the quantity that is to be produced.

Once the sales quantity has been determined, then the production quantity will be calculated as:

Sales quantity	X
Less opening inventories of finished goods	(X)
Add closing inventories of finished goods required	X
Production quantity	X

The opening inventories of finished goods are deducted from the sales quantity as we already have these in inventory and therefore do not need to make them.

Activity 2: Changes in inventory levels

A business has budgeted sales for the following period of 3,500 units of its product. The inventories at the start of the period are 800 units and these are to be reduced to 600 units at the end of the period.

Required

What is the production quantity for the period?

☐ units

3.2 Defective output

In many production processes, a certain percentage of finished goods will be defective and not saleable.

If there is an anticipated level of defective production, then the production quantity must be increased to ensure that there are enough units of the product available for sale after the defective products have been deducted. Therefore, the production quantity must be adjusted as follows:

Sales quantity	X
Less opening inventories of finished goods	(X)
Add closing inventories of finished goods required	X̲
Quantity required to meet sales demand	X
Add anticipated defective units	X̲
Production quantity	X̲

Activity 3: Defective output 1

Oliver Engineering's forecast sales quantities are as follows:

	Units			
Period 1	**Period 2**	**Period 3**	**Period 4**	**Period 5**
10,000	12,000	15,000	13,000	11,000

Each period is made up of four weeks, with five working days in each week.

Closing inventories of finished goods are to be enough to cover five days of sales demand for the next period.

Past experience has also shown that 2% of production is defective and has to be scrapped with no scrap value. The inventory of finished goods at the start of Period 1 is expected to be 3,000 units.

Required

Prepare production budgets for periods 1 to 4.

Activity 4: Defective output 2

A production process has normal losses of 5% of all completed output.

Required

If production of 4,200 good units is required, how many units must be produced in total?

[   ] units

4 Materials usage budget

The next stage is to determine the amount of material required for each unit of the product for the purposes of calculating the **materials usage budget**, and this will normally come from the standard cost card.

This quantity per unit will then be applied to the number of units to be produced, in order to determine the amount of material required to be used in production in each period.

4.1 Materials wastage

Wastage or **normal loss** of material must be taken into account when determining the amount of materials that are required in order to produce the quantity of products set out in the production budget.

Illustration 3: Materials usage budget

Continuing the Oliver Engineering example, we know that the production quantities required for each of the first four periods of the year are as follows:

Production budget – units

Period 1	Period 2	Period 3	Period 4
10,205	13,011	14,796	12,756

From the standard cost card, each unit of production requires 2 kg of material X. However, we also know that the production process has a normal loss of 20% of the materials input into the process.

This means that although each unit of product requires 2 kg of material X, this represents only 80% of the actual amount required. 20% more than 2 kg per unit must be inputted into the process.

The amount of material X required for each unit is therefore:

2 kg x 100/80 = 2.5 kg

The amount of normal loss can be calculated separately as:

$2 \text{ kg} \times \dfrac{20}{80} = 0.5 \text{ kg}$

The materials usage budget can now be prepared:

Materials usage budget

	Period 1	Period 2	Period 3	Period 4
Quantity of production	10,205	13,011	14,796	12,756
Materials usage (Quantity × 2.5 kg)	25,513 kg	32,528 kg	36,990 kg	31,890 kg

Activity 5: Wastage

A business requires 15,400 units of production in a period and each unit uses 5 kg of materials. The production process has a normal loss of 10% during the production process.

Required

What is the total amount of the material required for the period (to the nearest kg)?

☐ kg

5 Materials purchases budget

Once the materials usage budget has been set, then this can be translated into the **materials purchases budget** in units of materials and £.

Just as with the production budget, the opening and closing levels of materials inventories must be taken into account, in order to determine how many materials must be purchased during each period. The quantity of purchases will be determined as follows:

Materials usage	X
Less opening inventory of materials	(X)
Add closing inventory of materials	X
Quantity to be purchased	X

Finally, once the quantity to be purchased is known, then the anticipated purchase price can be applied to this to determine the materials purchases budget in terms of value.

Illustration 4: Materials purchases budget

We know the materials usage budget for Oliver Engineering is as follows:

Materials usage budget

	Period 1	Period 2	Period 3	Period 4
Materials usage	25,513 kg	32,528 kg	36,990 kg	31,890 kg

It is the policy of the company to hold enough materials to cover 10 days of the following period of production. The inventory level at the start of Period 1 is 12,000 kg of material and the materials usage in Period 5 is calculated as 28,000 kg.

First, we must determine the inventory levels of materials required at the end of each period. This has to be enough to cover 10 days out of the 20 days of production for the next period. The closing inventories of materials are as follows:

Period 1	32,528 kg × 10 days/20 days	=	16,264 kg
Period 2	36,990 kg × 10 days/20 days	=	18,495 kg
Period 3	31,890 kg × 10 days/20 days	=	15,945 kg
Period 4	28,000 kg × 10 days/20 days	=	14,000 kg

Now the materials purchases budget can be prepared, first in units.

Materials purchases budget – kg

	Period 1	Period 2	Period 3	Period 4
Materials usage	25,513	32,528	36,990	31,890
Less opening inventories of materials	(12,000)	(16,264)	(18,495)	(15,945)
Add closing inventories of materials	16,264	18,495	15,945	14,000
Materials to be purchased	29,777	34,759	34,440	29,945

The cost of each kg of material X has been, and will continue to be, £5. Therefore, the value of the materials purchases budget can also be set by taking the quantity to be purchased for each period and applying the unit price. For example, for Period 1, 29,777 kg must be purchased at a cost of £5 per kg = £148,885.

Materials purchases budget – £

Period 1 £	Period 2 £	Period 3 £	Period 4 £
148,885	173,795	172,200	149,725

Activity 6: Materials purchases budget

A business requires 124,000 litres of a material for its next month's production run. The material costs £2.60 per litre and current inventories are 14,000 litres. The business aims to increase its inventory levels by 15% by the end of the month.

Required

What is the budgeted cost of materials for the month?

£	

6 Labour usage budget

Once the production budget has been set, then it is necessary to determine the number of hours of labour that are required for the production level in the **labour usage budget** in hours. This can be determined by referring to the standard cost card, which will state the number of hours of labour required for each unit of product.

6.1 Idle time

Idle time is made up of hours for which employees are at work and for which they must be paid, but these hours are not spent in producing the products of the business.

Therefore, a greater number of hours will need to be paid for, over and above standard time, in order to produce the required number of units.

Illustration 5: Idle time

The standard cost card for the Stephenson, produced by Oliver Engineering, shows that the standard time for production of one unit is 1 Grade A labour hour. However, only 80% of the time paid for is productive, so there is 20% of idle time.

The number of hours that must be paid in total in order to produce one unit is:

1 hour × 100/80 = 1.25 hours

The idle time per product can be calculated as 1 hour × $\dfrac{20}{80}$ = 0.25 hours.

Production budget – units

	Period 1	Period 2	Period 3	Period 4
Quantity of production	10,205	13,011	14,796	12,756

Labour usage budget – hours

	Period 1	Period 2	Period 3	Period 4
Labour hours	12,756 hrs	16,264 hrs	18,495 hrs	15,945 hrs

Activity 7: Idle time

A product requires 10 labour hours for each unit. However, 10% of working hours are idle time.

Required

How long must an employee be paid for in order to produce 20 units (to the nearest hour)?

☐ Hours

7 Labour cost budget

Once we know the number of hours to be worked in each period, then the **labour cost budget** (in £) can be set by applying the wage rate to the number of hours. However, care must be taken with any overtime hours that are to be worked.

Illustration 6: Labour cost budget

The labour usage budget for Oliver Engineering is as follows:

Labour usage budget – hours

	Period 1	Period 2	Period 3	Period 4
Labour hours	12,756 hrs	16,264 hrs	18,495 hrs	15,945 hrs

The Grade A labour are paid at a rate of £9 per hour but only 16,000 hours can be worked within the normal working hours. Any hours above 16,000 are overtime hours that are paid at time and a third.

We will now produce the figures for the **labour cost budget**:

Period 1	12,756 hours × £9	£114,804
Period 2	(16,000 hours × £9) + (264 hours × £12)	£147,168
Period 3	(16,000 hours × £9) + (2,495 hours × £12)	£173,940
Period 4	15,945 hours × £9	£143,505

The labour cost budget will look like this:

Labour cost budget – £

Period 1	Period 2	Period 3	Period 4
£114,804	£147,168	£173,940	£143,505

7.1 Labour efficiency

Labour efficiency occurs when the workforce works more efficiently than the standard hours. Therefore, there will be fewer hours required for production than are indicated by the standard cost card.

> ### Illustration 7: Labour efficiency
>
> Let us suppose that a business is to produce 100,000 units of its product in a period and the standard cost card shows that each unit requires four labour hours.
>
> However, the workforce is producing at 110% efficiency.
>
> The number of hours of labour required to produce the 100,000 units will be calculated as follows:
>
> 100,000 units × 4 hours × 100/110 = 363,636 hours

Activity 8: Labour efficiency

A business wishes to produce 12,000 units of its product with a standard labour time of six hours per unit. However, the workforce is currently working at 120% efficiency.

Required

How long will it take to produce the units required?

☐ hours

8 Overheads budget

Budgets must also be set for the **overheads** and production facilities related costs, which can include, for example, factory rent and costs of running machinery. Overheads will also include depreciation charges.

As we have already seen in Chapter 1, overheads may be variable, semi-variable, fixed or stepped costs.

> ### Illustration 8: Overheads budget
>
> Oliver Engineering is now trying to produce estimates for its overheads for the first four periods of the year.

The cost of machine power is considered to be a true variable cost and it has been estimated that each Stephenson uses £2.40 of machine power.

The cost of the maintenance department has been estimated at £12,000 if 8,000 units are produced; and £16,000, if 12,000 units are produced.

The factory rent is £104,000 for each year.

The cost of production supervisors depends upon the level of activity within the factory. For an activity level of up to 12,000 units, the production supervisors' costs are £2,000 per period; for up to 14,000 units, this increases to £3,000; and for activity up to 16,000 units, the cost rises to £4,000 per period.

Before we can prepare the overhead budget, we must use the high low method to determine the variable and fixed elements of the maintenance department costs.

Maintenance department costs

	Production level	Total cost
	Units	£
Level 1	8,000	12,000
Level 2	12,000	16,000
Increase	4,000	4,000

Variable cost = £4,000/4,000 units = £1 per unit

At 8,000 units:

	£
Variable cost 8,000 × £1	8,000
Fixed element (bal fig)	4,000
Total cost	12,000

We can produce the budgeted figures for each of these overheads based as usual on the production budget:

Machine power is a variable cost = units × £2.40

Maintenance department is a semi-variable cost = (units × £1) + £4,000

Rent is a fixed cost = £104,000 × 4/52 = £8,000 per period

Supervisors' costs are a stepped cost:	≤ 12,000 units	= £2,000
	≤ 14,000 units	= £3,000
	≤ 16,000 units	= £4,000

Production budget – units

Period 1	Period 2	Period 3	Period 4
10,205	13,011	14,796	12,756

Overhead budget – £

	Period 1	Period 2	Period 3	Period 4
Machine power @ £2.40/unit	24,492	31,226	35,510	30,614
Maintenance department @ £1/unit + £4,000	14,205	17,011	18,796	16,756
Rent – £8,000 per period	8,000	8,000	8,000	8,000
Supervisors' costs	2,000	3,000	4,000	3,000
	48,697	59,237	66,306	58,370

9 Plant utilisation budget

The plant utilisation budget is a plan of the plant and machinery usage required for budgeted production.

Illustration 9: Plant utilisation budget

Company Y manufactures three products: A,B and C.

Product	Units	Machine hours per unit
A	500	1.5
B	380	2
C	750	0.5

There are three machines in the department. Additional machines can be hired if required. Each machine can be used for 500 hours in the month of December.

The machine hours needed to manufacture these in December are calculated as follows:

Product	Units	Hours per unit	Hours required
A	500	1.5	**750**
B	380	2	**760**
C	750	0.5	**375**
Total			**1,885**

3 machines, each operating for 500 hours = 1,500 machine hours. 1,885 hours are required, therefore **one** extra machine must be hired.

10 Preparing a budgeted operating statement

Having prepared detailed budgets, many organisations put them all together to produce a **budgeted operating statement** (ie budgeted profit and loss account down to operating profit) for the period in question. This provides managers with an overview of their expected performance.

A **master budget** is completed by adding a budgeted statement of financial position and a **cash budget**.

The statement of financial position reflects the assets and liabilities of the business. A full statement of financial position is unlikely to be tested but elements such as non-current assets could be tested. We consider non-current assets when looking at capital budgets later in this chapter.

Cash budgets will be considered in the next chapter.

Here we concentrate on the budgeted operating statement.

Illustration 10: Budgeted operating statement

Oliver Engineering now wants to produce a budgeted operating statement at the end of each of Periods 1 to 4. We will look at Period 1 here.

In the case of Oliver Engineering, opening and closing inventories of finished Stephensons are 3,000, so because there is no change in inventory levels, there is no need to include them in cost of sales. However, we know that there is a change in materials inventories from 12,000 at the start of Period 1, to 16,264 at the end of Period 1.

In the budgeted operating statement below, we have taken the materials used to produce the finished goods sold, at the cost of £5 per kg, as the cost of materials. This comes straight from the materials usage budget. When there are different prices for materials in inventory and purchased, a different approach is required. In such a case, we could have arrived at the figure as follows:

	£
Materials at start of Period 1 (12,000 kg x £5)	60,000
Materials purchased (29,777 kg x £5)	148,885
Less closing inventory of materials (16,264 kg x £5)	(81,320)
Cost of materials used	127,565

Oliver Engineering – budgeted operating statement for Period 1

	£	£
Revenue (from sales budget) 10,000 units × £40		400,000
Less cost of sales (10,205 units)		
Materials (from materials usage budget) 25,513 kg × £5	127,565	
Labour (from labour cost budget)	114,804	
Overheads (from overhead budget)	48,697	
		291,066
Budgeted gross profit for Period 1		108,934

Activity 9: Operating budget – Treble

You are drawing up the operating budget for the production of the Treble Ltd.

Production Budget	Units
Opening inventory of finished goods	3,000
Production	20,000
Sub-total	23,000
Sales	16,000
Closing inventory of finished goods	7,000

Required

(a) Complete these workings schedules

Materials	Kg	£
Opening inventory	2,000	4,750
Purchases	14,000	35,000
Sub-total	16,000	39,750
Used in production		
Closing inventory	1,000	

Closing inventory to be valued at budgeted purchase price

Labour	Hours	£
Basic time @ £8 per hour		
Overtime		
Total		

It take 15 minutes to make each item. 25 staff work 160 basic hours each in the period. Overtime is paid time and a half (50% above basic rate).

Overhead	Hours	£
Variable @ £2 per hour		
Fixed		7,750
Total		

Variable overhead is recovered on total labour hours

(b) **Complete the operating budget**

Enter income, costs and inventories as positive figures.

Closing inventory will be valued at the budgeted production cost per unit.

Use a negative figure to indicate a gross loss or an operating loss for example –500 or (500).

Operating budget	Units	£
Sales revenue @ £7.50 each	16,000	
Opening inventory of finished goods		13,500
Cost of production		
Materials		
Labour		
Overhead		
Total		
Closing inventory of finished goods*		
Cost of goods sold		
Gross profit		
Overheads		
Administration		7,000

Operating budget	Units	£
Marketing		10,000
Total		
Operating profit		

Assessment focus point

In an assessment, be careful not to include irrelevant data such as profits on the sale of non-current assets, or increases in administration overhead, within gross profit. These would alter the net profit, but feature after gross profit. The same principles apply regarding where to place various expenditure in a budgeted statement of profit or loss as to an actual one.

11 Capital budgets

A **capital budget** is a budget for the cost of non-current assets, ie for the purchase of non-current assets. Some non-current assets are purchased by one payment of the total cost. However, as non-current assets are major items of expenditure, payment for them may often be spread over a number of instalments. Most capital budgets will show these payments in the relevant periods.

Illustration 11: Capital budget

The senior management of Oliver Engineering have authorised the purchase of a new computer for the sales office and some new machinery. The computer has a cost of £2,500 and is to be paid for by cheque in Period 3. The machinery costs £500,000 and is to be paid for in instalments of £250,000 each in Period 1 and Period 4. We will now produce the capital budget.

	Period 1 £	Period 2 £	Period 3 £	Period 4 £
Computer			2,500	
Machinery	250,000			250,000
	250,000	–	2,500	250,000

12 Planning and agreeing draft budgets

In order to achieve budget integrity, the following steps should be taken.

- Draft budgets should be planned and then agreed with all parties. In Chapter 3, we considered the budget setting process, with budgets being reworked perhaps a number of times. The final version should be agreed by both the senior management and the manager of the responsibility centre concerned.

- Review of budgets. The managers of the responsibility centres should check and reconcile figures in the budget to ensure their accuracy and consistency. This may require revisions to the budget throughout the period to which it refers. Revisions may be required if actual results highlight an unrealistic plan or if the underlying forecasts or planning assumptions have to change because of external factors. The budgets must then be recalculated.

13 Sources of information

In Chapter 2, we looked at the sources of data for forecasting.

Such information is gathered from a wide variety of sources, which may be internal to the organisation itself, or external. The manager preparing his or her budget must be able to select the most valid and reliable source for the information he or she requires. A good budget will state the sources that have been used in its preparation.

Note that the terms 'data' and 'information' are used interchangeably here, although technically, data means unprocessed facts and figures, while information means data that has been processed into a useable form. Information for forecasting comes from both internal and external sources.

14 Threats to budget achievement

It is important to bear in mind here that one or all of the assumptions on which forecasts and related budgets are based may turn out to be incorrect. For example, due to economic or political conditions (including changes in taxation), materials and labour costs may rise more quickly than was assumed when the forecast and budget were constructed. Therefore, assumptions and sources of information used when creating forecasts and budgets should always be documented so that anyone using them is aware of the risks and uncertainties involved.

Once these have been agreed, the budget should be submitted for approval.

Chapter summary

- A standard costing system allows the standard cost of production to be compared to the actual costs and variances calculated.

- The use of standard costs complements budgets, together forming a system of planning and control.

- The direct materials standard cost is set by determining the estimated quantity to be used per unit and the estimated price per material unit.

- The direct labour standard cost is set by determining the estimated labour time per unit and the estimated rate per hour.

- The fixed overhead standard cost is determined by finding a realistic estimate of each of the elements of the fixed overhead. The standards that can be set include ideal standards, attainable standards and basic standards.

- The sales budget will normally be the first budget to be prepared, if it is the key budget factor, showing the anticipated sales in both units and value.

- From the sales budget, the production budget will be prepared, taking into account planned changes in inventory levels for finished goods and the anticipated level of defective finished goods.

- The production budget is then used to prepare the materials and labour budgets in terms of both units and value.

- The materials usage budget is based upon the production for the period but must take account of materials wastage during the production process.

- The materials purchases budget is based upon the materials usage budget but with adjustments for planned changes in inventories of materials – once the quantities of purchases are known, then they can be valued by applying the anticipated purchase price per unit.

- The labour usage budget is based upon the production budget and the standard hours for each unit. However, any idle time or labour efficiency must also be built into the number of hours required to complete the planned production. Once the hours have been determined, the labour cost budget can be calculated using the hourly rates of labour, taking account of any overtime hours required.

- Budgets will also be set for overheads – in order to try to estimate the expected overhead or expense, the behaviour of the cost must be taken into account: variable, semi-variable, fixed or stepped.

- Detailed budgets may be summarised into a budgeted operating statement (ie budgeted profit and loss account down to operating profit) for the period, in order to provide managers with an overview of their expected performance. If this is not acceptable, then they can plan to make adjustments to various areas of activity in order to try to meet their objectives.

- A master budget is completed by adding a budgeted statement of financial position and a cash budget to the budgeted operating statement.

- A capital budget will be prepared for planned expenditure on non-current assets.

Keywords

- **Attainable standards:** standards into which elements of normal wastage and inefficiency are built

- **Basic standards:** historical standards that are normally set when the product is initially produced

- **Budgeted operating statement:** a summary of the detailed budgets for the period, which provides managers with an overview of expected performance

- **Cash budget:** used to plan and control cash flow

- **Capital budget:** the expenditure planned on non-current assets

- **Efficiency:** the workforce is known to work more or less efficiently than the hours indicated by the standard cost card

- **Ideal standards:** standards set on the basis of perfect working conditions

- **Idle time:** non-productive hours that are worked and paid for

- **Labour usage budget:** (hours) the budget for the number of labour hours required for the planned level of production

- **Labour cost budget:** the cost of the labour hours required for the planned production

- **Master budget:** a summary budget comprising a budgeted operating statement, budgeted statement of financial position and a cash budget

- **Materials usage budget:** (units of materials) the budget for the units of materials to be used in the production process

- **Materials purchases budget:** (units and £) the budget for the quantity and value of materials purchases required

- **Normal loss:** the expected amount of lost production or material wastage through defective goods or the production process

- **Overheads budget:** the budget for indirect expenses of the business

- **Production budget:** (finished goods units) budget for the number of units of production

- **Standard costing system:** a system which assigns standard costs to each cost unit and allows a comparison of standard costs to actual costs and the calculation of variances

- **Variances:** the difference between the standard costs and the actual costs for a period

Activity answers

Activity 1: Ideal standards

Using an ideal standard for materials cost, which allows for no material wastage, will have a demotivating effect on workers, as even with the most careful working, they will never be able to achieve the materials usage reflected in this cost.

While the production manager is right to try to use the budget to improve the performance of workers, the budget must reflect realistic, although challenging, performance standards. It should therefore use an attainable standard instead, which might be based on the materials usage of the most experienced (and presumably least wasteful) workers, and so will incorporate a small amount of wastage.

Additionally, if an ideal standard is used, such that material usage will always be greater than budgeted, this could lead to production stoppages if insufficient material has been purchased to meet the actual usage, and it is difficult to source more at short notice.

Activity 2: Changes in inventory levels

The correct answer is: $\boxed{3,300}$ units

Workings

	Units
Sales	3,500
Less opening inventories of finished goods	(800)
Add closing inventories of finished goods	600
Production quantity	3,300

Activity 3: Defective output 1

The finished goods inventory levels are determined by finding five days of sales demand for the next period:

Period 1	12,000 units × 5 days/20 days	=	3,000 units
Period 2	15,000 units × 5 days/20 days	=	3,750 units
Period 3	13,000 units × 5 days/20 days	=	3,250 units
Period 4	11,000 units × 5 days/20 days	=	2,750 units

We can now start to forecast the production quantities that are required for the first four periods of next year.

Production budget – units

	Period 1	**Period 2**	**Period 3**	**Period 4**
Sales quantity	10,000	12,000	15,000	13,000
Less opening inventories	(3,000)	(3,000)	(3,750)	(3,250)
Add closing inventories	3,000	3,750	3,250	2,750
Production quantity	10,000	12,750	14,500	12,500

We must now recognise that not all of the production is good production and that it is anticipated that 2% of the production will be defective.

Therefore, for Period 1, we need 10,000 units after defectives as good production.

The 10,000 good units therefore represent 98% of total production; and defectives, 2% of total production.

The additional amount of production necessary in Period 1 is therefore:

10,000 units × 2/98 = 205 units

Therefore, in order to have 10,000 good units at the end of the production run, it will be necessary to produce 10,205 units.

We can now produce the final production budget for the next four periods:

Production budget – units

	Period 1	**Period 2**	**Period 3**	**Period 4**
Sales quantity	10,000	12,000	15,000	13,000
Less opening inventories	(3,000)	(3,000)	(3,750)	(3,250)
Add closing inventories	3,000	3,750	3,250	2,750
Good production quantity (98%)	10,000	12,750	14,500	12,500
Defective production (2%) (2/98 × 10,000 etc)	205	261	296	256
Total production quantity (100%)	10,205	13,011	14,796	12,756

Activity 4: Defective output 2

The correct answer is: 4,422 units

	%	Units
Good units	95	4,200
Anticipated defective units 4,200 × 5/95	5	222
Required production 4,200 × 100/95	100	4,422

Activity 5: Wastage

The correct answer is: 85,556 kg

	Kg
Kg required for production 5 × 15,400	77,000
Additional for normal loss 77,000 × 10/90	8,556
Required usage 15,400 × 5 × 100/90	85,556

Activity 6: Materials purchases budget

The correct answer is: £327,860

		Litres
Materials usage		124,000
Less opening inventory		(14,000)
Add closing inventory 14,000 × 1.15	16,100	
Materials purchases		126,100

Cost of purchases   126,100 × £2.60 = £327,680

Activity 7: Idle time

The correct answer is: 222 hours.

Standard time	20 units × 10 hours	200
Additional time	200 × 10/90	22
Total time required	20 × 10 × 100/90	222

Activity 8: Labour efficiency

The correct answer is: 60,000 hours.

Hours required   12,000 × 6 hours × 100/120   = 60,000 hours

Activity 9: Operating budget - Treble

Materials	Kg	£
Opening inventory	2,000	4,750
Purchases	14,000	35,000
Subtotal	16,000	39,750
Used	15,000	37,250
Closing inventory	1,000	2,500

Closing inventory to be valued at budgeted purchase price

Labour	Hours	£
Basic time @ £8 per hour	4,000	32,000
Overtime	1,000	12,000
Total	5,000	44,000

Overhead	Hours	£
Variable @ £2 per hour	5,000	10,000
Fixed		7,750
Total		17,750

Operating budget	Units	£
Sales revenue @ £7.50 each	16,000	120,000
Opening inventory of finished goods	3,000	13,500
Cost of production	20,000	
Materials		37,250
Labour		44,000
Overhead		17,750
Total		99,000
Closing inventory of finished goods*	7,000	34,650
Cost of goods sold		77,850
Gross profit		42,150
Overheads		
Administration		7,000
Marketing		10,000
Total		17,000
Operating profit		25,150

*Valued at budgeted production cost per unit

1 **Complete the following production budget for the product of an organisation.** Closing inventory is to be 30% of the next period's sales. Sales in Period 4 will be 4,200 units.

Units of product

	Period 1	Period 2	Period 3
Opening inventory	1,140		
Production			
Units required			
Sales	3,800	4,000	4,500
Closing inventory			
Units required			

2 For the organisation in the question above, quality control procedures have shown that 5% of the completed products are found to be defective and unsellable.

Complete the following:

Units of product

	Period 1	Period 2	Period 3
Production (from above)			
Actual production			

3 The production budget for Product B shows 12,000 units in Period 1 and 11,000 units in Period 2.

Each completed unit of the product requires 4 kg of material. However, the production process has a normal loss of 10% of materials input. Inventory levels of materials are held in order to be sufficient to cover 35% of actual usage for the following period. The materials held in inventory at the beginning of Period 1 are 18,600 kg.

The price of each kilogram of material is £4.80.

Complete the following for Period 1:

- The materials usage budget in units is ☐

- The materials purchases budget in units is ☐

- The materials purchases budget in £ is ☐

4   Budgeted sales of Product P for the next quarter are 42,000 units.

Finished goods in inventory at the start of the quarter are 7,000 units and closing inventory will be 8,334.

The standard cost card indicates that each unit should take 3.5 labour hours. However, it is anticipated that, due to technical problems during the quarter, the workforce will only be working at 92% efficiency.

The production budget for the quarter is [   ] units.

The labour usage budget for the quarter is [   ] hours.

5   The production budget is as follows:

Quarter 2	**Quarter 3**
16,020 units	17,850 units

The details of overheads are:

Light and heat – this is estimated at a rate of £4.80 per unit of production in each quarter.

Maintenance department – previous periods have shown that at a production level of 13,000 units, the maintenance department costs totalled £68,500; and at a production level of 17,000 units, the costs totalled £86,500.

Leased machinery – some of the machinery is leased, and for production levels up to 17,000 units, the leasing cost is £15,600 per quarter. However, if production exceeds this level, then a further machine must be leased at a quarterly cost of £4,800.

Rent and rates – the rent and rates are £84,000 per annum.

Complete the following:

Overhead budget

Overhead cost £	Quarter 2	Quarter 3
Light and heat		
Maintenance		
Leasing		
Rent and rates		

6   Sales of a product in the next four week period are expected to be 280 units. At the beginning of the period, 30 units is held in inventory, although the budgeted closing inventory is expected to be five units.

Each unit of the product requires two hours of Grade O labour and three hours of Grade R labour. Grade O labour is paid £15 per hour, whereas Grade R labour (16 workers) receive a guaranteed weekly wage of £280.

A unit of the product requires 7 kg of material. The expected price per kg of the material is £50.

For the following four week period, what is the:

(a) Production budget? [   ] units

(b) Materials usage budget? [   ] kg costing £ [   ]

(c) Labour cost budget? £ [   ]

7   Two products, J and K, are produced from the same material. The data below relates to Period 1.

(a)	Budgeted production	J	450 units
		K	710 units
(b)	Material requirements per unit	J	25 kg
		K	40 kg
(c)	Opening inventory of material	40,000 kg	
(d)	Closing inventory of material	27,359 kg	

The purchases budget (in kg) for Period 1 is [   ]

8   Two products, X and Y, are manufactured. Budgeted production levels in Period 7 are 420 units of X, and 590 units of Y.

Each X requires five labour hours; each Y, four labour hours.

There are 25 production workers, each of whom works a 35-hour week. There are five weeks in each period.

The rate of pay per hour for production employees is £10. Any overtime is paid at 125% of basic rate.

(a) What are the budgeted labour hours to be worked during Period 7, including any overtime? [   ] hours

(b) What is the cost of labour budget for Period 7? £ [   ]

9   Four different services are offered to clients. The budgeted figures for the coming year are as follows:

	Service 1	Service 2	Service 3	Service 4
Charge per hour to clients	£20	£25	£30	£40
Budgeted chargeable hours	10,584	6,804	5,292	7,560
Payment per hour to employee	£8	£10	£11	£14

Staff are expected to work a 35 hour week for 48 weeks per year. 10% of their time is non-chargeable. It is company policy to employ part-time staff (who work 17.5 hours per week for 48 weeks per year) as well as full-time staff, but a maximum of one part-time member of staff per service stream.

Complete the following (part time employees count as 0.5).

	Service 1	Service 2	Service 3	Service 4
Revenue budget (£)				
Number of employees				
Direct wages budget (£)				

Preparing cash budgets

5

Learning outcomes

2.6	Prepare cash flow forecasts
	• Prepare a cash flow forecast from budget data, making due allowance for time lags or assumptions about changes in debtor, creditor and inventory balances
	• Analyse a cash flow forecast into shorter control periods, allowing for time lags

Assessment context

Preparation of cash budgets is likely to be tested in the assessment where after producing an operating budget, a cash flow forecast may need to be prepared.

Qualification context

Preparation of cash budgets is also tested in *Cash and Treasury Management*.

Business context

Management of cash resources is very important for any business; accurate cash forecasting is part of this.

Chapter overview

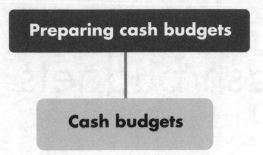

Preparing cash budgets

Cash budgets

Focus on 'cash effect'
question approach:

(1) One-offs/irregular, eg
Sale/purchase of non-
current assets

(2) Regular payments with no
timing effect

(3) Items with timing

	Mth 1	Mth 2	Mth 3
Cash receipts			
Cash payments			
Net cash flow			
Cash b/f			
Cash c/f			

Introduction

As you will be aware from your earlier studies, cash is as important to the survival of a business as profit. It follows, therefore, that management also needs to plan and control cash flows (in and out) – not just income and expenditure. This is done by preparing a cash budget.

Cash budgets can give management an indication of any cash surpluses or shortages expected.

Management can then make decisions on financing any expected cash shortage or investing any cash surpluses.

1 Cash budgets

Key term

The level of cash held by a business is important. A **cash budget** shows how the balance will change over several months.

1.1 Presentation of a cash budget

The net cash flow is determined by deducting the payments from the receipts and this net movement is applied to the opening cash balance in order to find the anticipated closing balance.

XYZ Ltd: Cash budget for the three months ended 31 March 20X7

	Jan	Feb	Mar
Cash receipts			
Sales receipts	X	X	X
Sale of non-current assets	X		
Loan		X	
	X	**X**	**X**
Cash payments			
Purchase payments	X	X	X
Wages	X	X	X
Overheads	X	X	X
Purchase of non-current assets		X	
	X	**X**	**X**
Net cash flow	X	(X)	X
Opening balance	X	X	(X)
Closing balance	**X**	**(X)**	**X**

1.2 Approach to completing a cash budget

Fill in the easy figures first.

(1) Sundry receipts and payments, for example, the purchase of non-current assets.

(2) Wages and salaries: usually paid when due.

(3) Sales receipts. Check the timing of the cash receipt – some sales may be for cash; others, for credit. For cash sales, the cash inflow will take place at the same time as the sale. Sales on credit means that the cash for the sale will be received at some point in time after the sale, which might be within the credit terms, typically 30 days or 60 days after the invoice date, or beyond this.

(4) Payments of purchases and overheads. Again, the timing of the payment needs to be considered carefully.

(5) For the general overheads, the depreciation charge must be removed, as this is a non-cash expense.

Cash budgets consider the cash element of business transactions, whereas the income statement (profit or loss account down to operating profit) records all transactions on an accruals basis, regardless of when cash is received or paid.

2 Forecasting cash receipts and cash payments

In this section, we look at two methods of deriving receipts and payments from the budgeted operating statement (operating budget):

(1) Using the operating budget and changes in statement of financial position balances

(2) Using the operating budget and allowing for time lags

2.1 Using the operating budget and statement of financial position

Assessment focus point

You may need to work out the cash effect of a transaction from the operating budget and assumptions about changes in statement of financial position balances.

Sales recorded in a month will not usually equal cash received for that month, because most businesses will have a mixture of cash sales and sales on credit.

Therefore, some cash will not be received until after that month.

If business sales include credit sales, the cash received in a month is calculated by adjusting the sales figure by the change in the receivables balance.

Illustration 1: Cash budget 1

The cash received and cash paid for January can be worked out from the operating budget and assumptions on the change in the receivables balance as follows:

	£
Receivables b/fwd per statement of financial position	450
Sales (on credit) per operating budget	1,200
Receivables c/fwd per statement of financial position	(500)
Cash received	1,150

This can also be expressed as:

	£
Sales (on credit) per operating budget	1,200
Increase in receivables – from start to end of month per statement of financial position	(50)
Cash received	1,150

The same method applies to cash paid.

Purchase payments

	£
Payables b/fwd per statement of financial position	340
Purchases (on credit) per operating budget	760
Payables c/fwd per statement of financial position	(320)
Cash paid	780

This can also be expressed as:

	£
Purchases (on credit) per operating statement	760
Increase in payables – from start to end of month per statement of financial position	20
Cash received	780

2.2 Using the operating budget and allowing for time lags

From the total budget sales, a certain amount, either reported as an absolute amount or as a percentage of total sales, will be cash sales, and the remainder will be credit sales. As we have discussed earlier, cash received for cash sales are received at the time of sale.

For credit sales, the receipt of payment occurs at a time after the sale; there is a **time lag** between the sale and receipt of payment. We need to account for lagged payments and receipts, therefore assumptions are made about the time lag between the sales/purchases and cash received/paid.

Illustration 2: Cash budget 2

The fuel division of SC Fuel and Glass is preparing its quarterly cash flow forecast for the three months of October, November and December.

The sales of the fuel division for these three months are expected to be as follows:

October	£680,000
November	£700,000
December	£750,000

Of these sales, 20% are cash sales and the remainder are sales on credit. Experience has shown that, on average, the receivables for credit sales pay the money according to the following pattern:

The month after sale	20%
Two months after sale	50%
Three months after sale	30%

Therefore, the cash for October credit sales will be received in November, December and January. If we are preparing the cash flow forecast for the period from October to December, then some of the cash inflows will be from credit sales in earlier months. Therefore, you also require information about the credit sales for these earlier months.

The total sales in July to September for the fuel division (again 20% of these were cash sales) are:

July	£600,000
August	£560,000
September	£620,000

We can now start to piece together the information required to prepare the cash budget from sales for October to December:

Cash budget – October to December

	October £	November £	December £
Cash receipts:			
Cash sales			
(20% of month sales)	136,000	140,000	150,000

Now we need to deal with sales on credit, which are more complicated and will require a working:

Workings – Cash from credit sales

	October £	November £	December £
July sales			
(80% × 600,000 × 30%)	144,000		
August sales			
(80% × 560,000 × 50%)	224,000		
(80% × 560,000 × 30%)		134,400	
September sales			
(80% × 620,000 × 20%)	99,200		
(80% × 620,000 × 50%)		248,000	
(80% × 620,000 × 30%)			148,800
October sales			
(80% × 680,000 × 20%)		108,800	
(80% × 680,000 × 50%)			272,000
November sales			
(80% × 700,000 × 20%)			112,000
Cash from credit sales	467,200	491,200	532,800

Cash budget – October to December

	October £	November £	December £
Cash receipts:			
Cash sales	136,000	140,000	150,000
Cash from credit sales	467,200	491,200	532,800

Activity 1: Cash budget – Kookaburra

Kookaburra has prepared the following budgeted data.

	March	April	May	June	July
Sales	4,250	4,600	5,000	5,350	5,400
Purchases	1,200	1,300	1,500	1,600	1,750
Wages	800	800	850	850	850
Other overheads	650	650	675	675	675
Capital expenditure			3,000	1,000	

Additional information:

- 30% sales are for cash. The remaining sales are on credit and customers pay one month later.

- Purchases are paid for after one month.

- Wages and other overheads are paid in the current month. Other overheads include £400 of depreciation each month.

Required

Prepare a monthly cash flow forecast for Quarter 2.

	April	May	June	Total Qtr 2
Receipts				
Cash Sales				
Credit Sales				
Total Receipts				
Payments				
Purchases				
Wages				
Other overheads				
Capital expenditure				
Total payments				
Net Cash				
Opening cash balance	750			
Closing cash balance				

Activity 2: Cash budget – Aqua Ltd

Aqua Ltd is trying to forecast its cash position. Its operating budget is as follows:

Operating budget	£	£
Sales revenue		43,250
Expenditure		
Materials	12,500	
Labour	15,000	
Other costs	4,250	31,750
Operating profit		11,500

Aqua has made the following statement of financial position assumptions:

- Receivables will decrease by £2,300.
- Material payables will increase by £1,400.
- Labour costs are paid in the period in which they are incurred.
- Other payables will decrease by £900.

Required

Prepare the cash flow forecast from the operating budget and statement of financial position assumptions. Enter receipts and payments as positive figures.

Cash flow forecast	£	£
Sales receipts		
Payments		
Materials		
Labour		
Other costs		
Cash flow		

Show a net cash outflow as a negative, for example, –500.

3 Non-current assets and cash receipts or payments

When making capital purchases, the cash outflow often matches the amount shown as an addition in the statement of financial position. Alternatively, the payment may be made in instalments.

However, on the sale of an asset, the profit (or loss) that is recorded in the statement of profit or loss is not a cash amount. For the purposes of your cash budget, you may have to calculate the proceeds on sale. This can be done using the profit (or loss), provided you know the carrying amount of the asset in the books of the business (ie in the statement of financial position) at the date of sale.

Cash inflows on sale of non-current assets = proceeds

Proceeds =   Carrying amount (ie net book value)
                  plus
                  Profit on sale (or minus loss)

Activity 3: Sale of a non-current asset

AC Ltd sold machinery in February for a profit of £5,000. The carrying amount in February was £20,000.

Required

What were the proceeds from the sale of the machinery?

The proceeds were £ [   ]

BPP
LEARNING MEDIA

Chapter summary

- A cash budget or cash flow forecast allows an organisation to plan and control future cash flows in and out, and the expected cash or overdraft balance at the end of future periods.

- Receipts from cash sales will take place at the same time as the sale, but receipts from credit sales may be spread over a number of subsequent months.

- The movement in receivables during a period can be used with the budgeted sales to find the budgeted cash inflow (receipts) from sales during the period.

- Payments for purchases on credit will similarly be typically spread over a number of future months.

- The movement in payables during a period can be used with the budgeted purchases to find the budgeted cash outflow (payment) for purchases during the period.

- Any non-cash flows such as depreciation charges must be excluded from the cash flow forecast.

- The proceeds on the sale of non-current assets can be found by adding the profit on sale to (or by subtracting the loss on sale from) the carrying amount of the asset.

Keywords

- **Cash budget:** (also called cash flow forecast) method of determining the expected net cash flow for a future period and the expected cash or overdraft balance at the end of that future period

- **Time lag:** the time between the receipt/payment of cash and the related sale/purchase

- **Net cash flow:** determined by deducting the payments from the receipts and this net movement is applied to the opening cash balance in order to find the anticipated closing balance

Activity answers

Activity 1: Cash budget – Kookaraba
Monthly cash flow forecast for Quarter 2

	April	May	June	Total Qtr 2
Receipts				
Cash Sales	1,380	1,500	1,605	4,485
Credit Sales	2,975	3,220	3,500	9,695
Total Receipts	4,355	4,720	5,105	14,180
Payments				
Purchases	1,200	1,300	1,500	4,000
Wages	800	850	850	2,500
Other overheads	250	275	275	800
Capital expenditure	–	3,000	1,000	4,000
Total payments	2,250	5,425	3,625	11,300
Net Cash	2,105	(705)	1,480	2,880
Opening cash balance	750	2,855	2,150	750
Closing cash balance	2,855	2,150	3,630	3,630

Activity 2: Cash budget – Aqua Ltd

Cash flow forecast	£	£
Sales receipts		45,550
Payments		
Materials	11,100	
Labour	15,000	
Other costs	5,150	31,250
Cash flow		14,300

BPP
LEARNING MEDIA

Activity 3: Sale of non-current asset

The sales proceeds were £ | **25,000** |

Profit + carrying amount = 5,000 + 20,000 = £25,000

Test your learning

1 A business has estimates of the following sales figures:

	£
October	790,000
November	750,000
December	720,000
January	700,000
February	730,000
March	760,000

Of these total sales figures, 10% are likely to be cash sales and the remainder are credit sales. The payment pattern from receivables in the past has been such that 40% of the total sales pay in the month after the sale; and the remainder, two months after the month of sale. However, there are also normally 5% irrecoverable debts.

Complete the following.

	January	February	March
Budgeted cash receipts from sales (£)			

2 A business has estimates of the following sales figures:

	£
October	790,000
November	750,000
December	720,000
January	700,000
February	730,000
March	760,000

The business operates at a standard gross profit margin of 25%. Purchases are all made in the same month as the sale and are all on credit. 20% of purchases are offered a 2% discount for payment in the month after purchase and the business takes all such discounts. A further 65% of the purchases are paid for two months after the month of purchase; and the remaining 15% are paid for three months after the date of purchase.

Complete the following.

	January	February	March
Budgeted cash payments for purchases (£)			

3   A business is about to prepare a cash flow forecast for the quarter ending 31 December.

Gross wages are expected to be £42,000 each month and are paid in the month during which they are incurred. General overheads are anticipated to be £30,000 for each of September and October, increasing to £36,000 thereafter. 80% of the general overheads are paid for in the month during which they are incurred; and the remainder, the following month. Included in the general overheads figure is a depreciation charge of £5,000 each month.

The business has planned to purchase new equipment for £40,000 in November; and in the same month, to dispose of old equipment, with estimated sales proceeds of £4,000.

Complete the following extracts from the cash budget for the three months ending 31 December.

	October £	November £	December £
Cash receipts:			
Sales proceeds from equipment			
Cash payments:			
Wages			
General overheads			
New equipment			

4   Make-it Ltd intends to sell an industrial unit, making a budgeted profit of £58,000. The carrying amount of the unit is £212,000. **What are the budgeted cash inflows on the sale of the unit ie the proceeds?**

Select from:

(a)   £58,000
(b)   £154,000
(c)   £212,000
(d)   £270,000

Budget preparation
– limiting factors

6

Learning outcomes

2.2	Identify and calculate the effect of production and sales constraints
	• Identify budget limiting factors, for example, a production bottleneck, possible market share or access to finance
	• Calculate the production limit.

Assessment context

Identifying and calculating the impacts of constraints on budgets, or making suggestions for how to deal with the constraints given, are likely to be examined.

Qualification context

Limiting factors are tested in both *Budgeting* and *Decision and Control* at Level 4.

Business context

A core part of any business is to determine its objectives and come up with a plan of how they will achieve these objectives (strategy). Budgeting provides detail of how the business should operate in order to achieve its objectives, given the effect of production and sales constraints.

Chapter overview

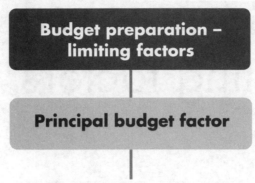

Budget preparation – limiting factors

Principal budget factor

The factor which limits the activities of the organisation – production budgets should reflect these constraints

Optimising contribution

Approach:

(1) Calculate contribution per unit

(2) Calculate contribution per unit of limiting factor (contribution/ unit ÷ kg or hours/unit)

(3) Rank products

(4) Prepare optimal production plan

(5) Prepare remaining budgets

Introduction

In this chapter, we will look at various **limiting factors** which dictate budget construction. We will cover: resources as limiting factors; maximising contribution; product mix and 'buying in'.

1 Resources as limiting factors

We looked at the **key budget factor** earlier in this Course Book. This is the element or resource of the business that is likely to place limitations on the activities of the business.

In most businesses, the key budget factor will be sales. However, it is also possible that the key budget factor may be dictated by resources: the availability of materials, labour or machine capacity. We consider these cases in this chapter.

2 Shortage of materials

In a manufacturing organisation, the sales demand for a product may be virtually unlimited. However, there may be a shortage of materials availability, which will then become the factor that limits production volume.

Illustration 1: Shortage of materials

SS Productions makes a single product for which each unit requires 3.5 kg of material LP1. Unfortunately, due to a shortage of suppliers of LP1, only 525,000 kg of LP1 will be available in the coming year, with supplies being available on a monthly basis, spread evenly over the year.

How many units of the product can be produced in total and each month?

Total production   = $\dfrac{525,000 \text{ kg}}{3.5 \text{ kg}}$

            =   150,000 units

Monthly production   = $\dfrac{150,000}{12}$

            =   12,500 units

2.1 Solving the problem of shortage of materials

The shortage of supply may be a long-term problem or it may only be a short-term blip. Possible longer term solutions include the following:

- **Seeking an alternative supplier** – this is an obvious solution but it may not always be possible to find another supplier who can supply the correct quality at an acceptable price.

- **Finding an alternative material** – in some instances, a product can only be made from one particular material but it may be possible to adapt the

design of the product and the manufacturing process in order to use a substitute material that is widely available.

- **Manufacturing an alternative product** – it may be possible to switch the production process to manufacture an alternative product which uses a different material that is not in short supply.

- **Buying in finished goods for resale** – instead of producing the product, it could be purchased in finished form from another producer who is not having the same problems with supply of the materials required. However, this would probably lead to an under-utilisation of production resources and a major change in organisational strategy.

If the shortage is only temporary, then there are a number of short-term solutions that could alleviate the problem:

- **Using materials held in inventory** – the inventories of materials could be run down in order to maintain production and sales.

- **Using finished goods held in inventory** – in order to maintain sales in the short term, finished goods inventories can be run down, even though production levels are not as high as would be liked.

- **Rescheduling purchases** – if the amount of the material required is available in some periods but not in others, then the materials purchases could be rescheduled to ensure that the maximum use is made of the available materials.

Illustration 2: Shortage of materials 2

The materials requirements for production for Selby Electronics for the next six months are as follows:

	May	June	July	Aug	Sep	Oct
Materials requirements – kg	4,500	5,000	5,200	4,800	5,400	6,000

Selby is only able to purchase 5,000 kg of the material each month.

How can the purchases be scheduled in order to ensure the maximum production over the six month period?

In total, over the six month period 30,900 kg of material is required, whereas only 30,000 kg is available. Therefore, there will be a shortage of 900 kg which will have to be dealt with by possibly finding another supplier.

If only the amount required for production is purchased each month, and 5,000 kg is purchased in months where the requirements are higher than this, then only 29,300 kg will be purchased, meaning that there will be an overall shortage of 1,600 kg (30,900 – 29,300).

However, instead of purchasing what is required for production each month, if all of the available 5,000 kg are purchased every month, then the shortage can be reduced to just 900 kg (30,900–30,000). This will mean holding higher inventory levels of the material, however, which will incur extra costs.

This can be illustrated in the schedule below – on this basis, production can be completed in full in every month other than October.

	May	Jun	Jul	Aug	Sep	Oct
Materials requirements – kg	4,500	5,000	5,200	4,800	5,400	6,000
Materials purchased – kg	5,000	5,000	5,000	5,000	5,000	5,000
(Shortage)/excess	500	–	(200)	200	(400)	(1,000)
Rescheduled purchases	(500)		200	(200)	400	100
Shortage after rescheduling	–	–	–	–	–	900

Activity 1: Shortage of materials

A production process requires 7.5 kg of material per unit of production. For the first three months of next year, only 165,000 kg of material will be available each month.

Required

Assuming production is spread evenly over the three months, what will the maximum monthly production level be?

3 Labour shortages

In some instances, the key budget factor might be the availability of labour with the correct skills or training. In this case, the number of hours available will determine the quantity of production.

Illustration 3: Labour shortages

Poldark Engineering requires a particular grade of skilled labour for one of its products. Each product requires four hours of this grade of labour but the business currently only has 20 employees with the skills required. They normally work a 35 hour week, although by paying an overtime rate of double time, it has been possible to negotiate for each employee to work 10 hours of overtime a week.

What is the maximum level of production each week?

Hours available	=	$20 \times (35 + 10)$
	=	900 hours per week
Maximum production	=	$\dfrac{900 \text{ hours}}{4 \text{ hours}}$
	=	225 units per week

3.1 Solving the problem of a shortage of labour

Labour shortage problems are normally fairly short-term, as it should be possible to obtain more of the labour required, either by paying higher wages or by investing in employee training. There are a number of short-term solutions, however, that could be used to alleviate the problem until it can be resolved:

- **Increase the overtime worked** – it may be possible to agree additional overtime with the employees in order to maintain production levels.

- **Use sub-contractors** – in some types of business, it may be possible to use agency workers or to sub-contract the work in order to maintain production levels. Either of these options is likely to be fairly costly.

- **Use up finished goods held in inventory** – if production levels are reduced, then for the short term, sales can still be maintained by running down the finished goods inventory.

- **Buying in finished goods inventory** – this could be an expensive option, leaving factory capacity under-utilised and may have quality implications as well.

- **Improving labour efficiency** – this is not something that can be done quickly but with training and over a period of time, it may be possible.

Activity 2: Labour shortages

In the first week of the next quarter, sales demand is expected to be 2,000 units of a product. Each unit requires 5.5 hours of direct labour time and the business employs 280 employees, each working a 35 hour week.

Required

How much overtime (to the nearest 0.1 hours per week) would each employee need to work in order to meet demand with the current workforce?

| | hours per week

4 Lack of production capacity

It is also possible for a lack of production capacity in terms of machinery or floor space in the factory to be the key budget factor. In this case, the production level will be dependent upon the maximum capacity of the factory.

Illustration 4: Lack of production capacity

Henley Engineering operates out of one factory and operates two eight hour shifts each day for six days a week, with the production line working at full capacity. The production line is capable of producing 100 units of product per hour.

What is the maximum production level each week?

Total hours	=	$2 \times 8 \times 6$
	=	96 hours
Maximum production	=	96 hours × 100 units
	=	9,600 units

4.1 Solving capacity problems

Capacity problems mean that the current operations are not sufficient to meet demand for the product from customers. These problems may be short-term or long-term.

If the capacity problem is short-term, such as the problem of dealing with high seasonal demand, there are a number of possible short-term solutions:

- **Build up inventories in advance** – if the high demand is known or expected in advance, then given that this is a seasonal problem, production could be higher in the months before high demand is expected and finished goods inventories would grow, ready to meet the greater demand. There will obviously be costs involved in holding higher levels of finished goods in inventory.

- **Additional shifts** – it may be possible for staff to work additional shifts in order to increase capacity. However, this could cause substantial overtime costs.

- **Buying in finished goods** – in order to meet the additional demand in the short term, it may be possible to buy in the finished goods rather than to produce them

- **Renting equipment or premises** – it may be possible to rent temporary equipment or premises in order meet the short-term excess demand.

Long-term capacity shortages are usually resolved by investing in long-term non-current assets and increasing the shifts and/or number of workers.

5 Maximising contribution

As fixed costs in total are assumed to be constant, whatever combination of product is made, maximisation of profit will be achieved by maximising **contribution**. The contribution per unit is the sales price, less the variable costs per unit (usually materials and labour).

If a business has more than one product, and one limiting factor, the technique to use in order to maximise contribution is to determine the contribution per unit of the scarce resource or limiting factor and concentrate first upon the production of the product with the highest contribution per limiting factor unit.

Illustration 5: Maximising contribution

Farnham Engineering makes three products A, B and C. The costs and selling prices of the three products are as follows:

	A	**B**	**C**
	£	£	£
Direct materials @ £4 per kg	8	16	12
Direct labour @ £7 per hour	7	21	14
Variable overheads	3	9	6
Marginal cost	18	46	32
Selling price	22	54	39
Contribution	4	8	7

Sales demand for the coming period is expected to be as follows:

Product A   3,000 units
Product B   7,000 units
Product C   5,000 units

The supply of materials is limited to 50,000 kg during the period; and the labour hours available are 28,000.

Step 1

Determine if there is a limiting factor other than sales demand. Consider the materials usage for each product if the maximum sales demand is produced. (You are not given the actual usage of materials of each product but you can work it out – for example, the materials cost for A is £8 and as the materials are £4 per kg, product A must use 2 kg etc.)

	A	**B**	**C**	**Total**
Materials (Demand × 2/4/3/kg)	6,000 kg	28,000 kg	15,000 kg	49,000 kg
Labour (Demand × 1/3/2 hrs)	3,000 hours	21,000 hours	10,000 hours	34,000 hours

As 50,000 kg of materials are available for the period and only 49,000 kg are required for the maximum production level, materials are not a limiting factor.

However, only 28,000 labour hours are available, whereas in order to meet the maximum demand, 34,000 hours are required. Therefore, labour hours are the limiting factor.

Step 2

Calculate the contribution per limiting factor unit – in this case, the contribution per labour hour – for each product. Then rank the products according to how high the contribution per labour hour is for each one.

	A	**B**	**C**
Contribution	£4	£8	£7
Labour hours per unit	1 hour	3 hours	2 hours
Contribution per labour hour			
£4/1	£4.00		
£8/3		£2.67	
£7/2			£3.50
Ranking	1	3	2

Product A makes the most contribution per unit of scarce resource (labour hours) so in order to maximise contribution, we must concentrate first on production of A up to its maximum sales demand (3,000 units), then on C up to its maximum sales demand (5,000 units), and finally, if there are any remaining hours available, on B.

Step 3

Construct the optimal production plan.

The optimal production plan in order to maximise contribution is:

	Units produced	Labour hours required
A	3,000	3,000
C	5,000	10,000
B (balance)	5,000 (W1)	15,000 (balancing figure)
		28,000

W1:

After making A and C, there are 15,000 hours left. Each unit of B needs three hours, so there is sufficient to make 15,000/3 = 5,000 units.

The contribution earned from this production plan is:

		£
A	(3,000 × £4)	12,000
B	(5,000 × £8)	40,000
C	(5,000 × £7)	35,000
Total contribution		87,000

Activity 3: Limiting factors: Robin Ltd

The data for two products manufactured by Robin Ltd is as follows:

	A	B
Material per unit	6 kg	8 kg
Labour per unit	1 hr	2 hrs
Maximum demand	2,150 units	1,800 units
Selling price/unit	£15	£20
Direct material cost/unit	£3	£4
Direct labour cost/unit	£2	£4
Inventory of finished goods:		
Opening	200	100
Closing	50	–

Maximum availability of materials is 27,000 kg and of labour is 5,000 hours.

Required

(a) **Identify the limiting factor.**
(b) **Prioritise the two products.**
(c) **Prepare the sales and production budgets**

(a) The limiting factor is [   ]

(b) Product [   ] would take priority over Product [   ]

(c) Production budget for Product A is [   ] and Product B is [   ]

Budgets

Optimum Production Plan

Product	Units	Hours/Unit	Hours available
			5,000
A			( )
B	∴		( )
Total			–

Sales budget for Product A is [   ] Product B is [   ] units.

Total budgeted sales revenue is: [   ]

Sales Budget

	Product A	Product B	Total
Production			
Add opening inventory			
Less closing inventory			
Sales (units)			
Selling price			
Revenue			

6 Buying in

Another possible scenario is for the organisation to stop production of one product completely and instead 'buy it in' from a supplier or sub-contractor. This strategy may be cheaper, and it will also free up production capacity in-house for other products.

When faced with decisions such as this, we take a marginal costing approach, looking initially at the difference between the contribution per unit of producing in-house and sub-contracting, and then at the changes in fixed costs that could occur.

Illustration 6: Buying in

Mammon Ltd currently produces 'Ards' in-house at a variable cost of £20 per unit. They sell for £55 per unit, and £15,500 per month of fixed overheads are attributed to them. Each month, 1,000 Ards are produced and sold, but this quantity is expected to fall soon (without affecting cost estimates).

A sub-contractor can produce Ards at a cost to Mammon Ltd of £25 per unit. The managing director of Mammon Ltd estimates that by sub-contracting, £3,000 of monthly fixed overheads will be saved.

What should Mammon Ltd do?

First of all, we calculate the contribution per unit on each of the two scenarios.

	In-house production £ per unit	Sub-contract £ per unit
Revenue	55.00	55.00
Variable cost	20.00	25.00
Contribution per unit	35.00	30.00

On this analysis, if production is sub-contracted, contribution falls by £5 per unit, or £5 × 1,000 = £5,000 per month. However, we are also told that £3,000 of monthly overhead will be saved, so in total there would be a decrease of (£5,000 – £3,000) = £2,000 of gross profit per month, or (£2,000/1,000) = £2 per unit.

If production and sales were estimated to continue at current levels, the decision would be to continue to make Ards in-house, unless the capacity can be used to produce items with higher profitability.

But production and sales are estimated to fall in the future, which would make it harder for Mammon to recover the fixed costs of in-house production. As a result, although sub-contracting involves additional variable costs, it may become more attractive at lower levels of output because of the saving in fixed costs.

We need to identify the level of sales/production at which we would be indifferent between making the product in-house and sub-contracting.

This will be where the additional variable costs incurred by buying in equal the savings in fixed costs.

Cost estimates do not change at different levels of production, so the difference between our variable costs and the cost of buying in (£25 – £20) = £5 per unit. As the monthly savings on fixed costs by sub-contracting production are £3,000, if we produced and sold £3,000/£5 = 600 Ards we would be indifferent as to whether to make or buy. At more than 600 units, we would want to continue making Ards; at less than 600, we would want to sub-contract. This can be shown as follows:

		Produce in-house £	Sub-contract £
650 units:			
Contribution	(650 × £35)	22,750	
	(650 × £30)		19,500
Fixed costs		(15,500)	(12,500)
		7,250	7,000
600 units:			
Contribution	(600 × £35)	21,000	
	(600 × £30)		18,000
Fixed costs		(15,500)	(12,500)
		5,500	5,500
550 units:			
Contribution	(550 × £35)	19,250	
	(550 × £30)		16,500
Fixed costs		(15,500)	(12,500)
		3,750	4,000

The decision rests with the managers of Mammon Ltd, and depends on what level of production and sales they estimate will be experienced.

Chapter summary

- Normally, production is limited by sales demand. However, in some instances, a resource such as the availability of material, labour hours or machine hours is the limiting factor.

- It may be possible to take actions to counter material, labour and production capacity shortages.

- If this cannot be done, an alternative strategy – where there is more than one product and a limiting factor – is to maximise overall profit by concentrating production on the products with the highest contribution per limiting factor unit.

- Alternatively, a decision may be made to 'buy in' a product or component, rather than manufacture in-house.

- In a make or buy decision with no limiting factors, the relevant costs are the differential costs between the two options. Typically, this includes any variable costs incurred/saved as a result of the decision and any savings in attributable fixed costs.

Keywords

- **Contribution:** sales revenue or selling price per unit, less variable costs
- **Key budget factor:** the element or resource of the business that is likely to place limitations on its activities
- **Limiting factor:** a factor of production or sales that limits the amount of a product that can be produced or sold

Activity 1: Shortage of materials

The correct answer is ⬚ 22,000 ⬚ units

Working

Maximum production level = $\dfrac{165,000 \text{ kg}}{7.5 \text{ kg}}$

= 22,000 units

Activity 2: Labour shortages

The correct answer is ⬚ 4.3 ⬚ hours per week

Working

Hours required 2,000 × 5.5	11,000
Hours currently available 280 × 35	9,800
Overtime hours required	1,200

Overtime per employee $= \dfrac{1,200}{280} = 4.3$ hours per week

Activity 3: Limiting factors: Robin Ltd

(a)   The limiting factor is **labour**

Required production budget	A	B	Total
Less opening inventory	(200)	(100)	
Add opening inventory	50	–	
Demand	2,150	1,800	
Required production to meet demand	2,000	1,700	
Materials required	6 kg	8 kg	
	12,000 kg	13,600 kg	25,600 kg
Labour required	1 hour	2 hours	
	2,000 hrs	3,400 hrs	5,400 hrs

∴ **labour is the limiting factor**

Contribution per unit	£10	£12	
Contribution per labour hour	£10	£6	
Ranking	1	2	

(b)   Product | **A** | would take priority over Product | **B** |

(c)

Budgets

Optimum Production Plan

Product	Units	Hours/Unit	Hours available
			5,000
A	2,000	1	(2,000)
B	∴ 1,500	2	(3,000)
Total	3,500		–

Production budget for Product A is | **2,000** | units and
Product B is | **1,500** | units.

	Product A	Product B	Total
Production	2,000	1,500	
Add opening inventory	200	100	
Less closing inventory	50	0	
Sales (units)	**2,150**	**1,600**	
Selling price	£15	£20	
Revenue	£32,250	£32,000	**£64,250**

1   The materials requirements for production for the next six months for a business are as follows:

	Jan	Feb	Mar	Apr	May	Jun
Materials requirements – kg	2,600	3,100	3,000	3,100	2,800	3,200

It is only possible to purchase 3,000 kg of the product each month.

How many kg of the material should be purchased each month in order to maximise production, assuming the minimum levels of material held in inventory are maintained?

2   For the next few months, a business foresees having a shortage of highly skilled labour for its production process. This is due to a recent increase in sales, which is expected to continue.

What options does the business have to alleviate this problem?

3   Over the coming weeks, a business foresees having a shortage of the appropriate quality material for its production process. This is due to a short-term supply issue which is not expected to continue.

What options does the business have to alleviate this problem?

4   A product requires 0.5 kg of material per unit and 24 minutes labour per unit. The demand for the product is 15,000 units per month.

Available material = 9,000 kg per month

There are 30 workers available to work on this product, each working 180 hours a month.

The limiting factor is [▼   ]

Picklist:

labour hours
material
sales demand

5   The following two products use the same material. The cost of the material is £2 per kg, and the cost of labour is £10 per hour.

Per unit	Product A	Product B
Sales price £	13	8
Direct materials kg	2	1.5
Direct labour hours	0.5	0.25
Variable overhead £	1	0.5

Labour hours are limited. **Tick the product which should be manufactured if profit is to be maximised.**

Product	Manufactured to maximise profit
Product A	
Product B	

Budgetary control – comparing budget and actual costs

7

Learning outcomes

3.5	**Integrate standard costing into budgetary control**
	• Use standard costing methodology to split the total material and the total labour variances into price and efficiency variances

3.6	**Prepare and explain a flexed budget**
	• Flex budgets, adjusting each element of the budget correctly according to the original budget assumptions about cost behaviour
	• Explain the purpose of budget flexing
	• Discuss the limitations of flexing in the context of a given scenario

3.7	**Calculate variances between budget and actual income and expenditure**
	• Calculate variances in absolute and percentage terms
	• Identify favourable and adverse variances
	• Compare like with like and present the results clearly

3.8	**Review and revise budgets to reflect changing circumstances**
	• Identify when a budget revision is appropriate
	• Calculate the impact of changes to planning assumptions and forecasts
	• Recalculate budgets accordingly

4.3	**Analyse variances and explain their impact on the organisation**
	• Identify significant variances
	• Use operational information provided to explain the likely causes of variances
	• Provide suitable advice to management
	• Explain the impact of variances on overall organisational performance
	• Identify where further investigation is needed
	• Make recommendations to improve operational performance

4.4	**Effectively present budgetary issues to management**
	• Identify and describe important budgetary planning and control issues
	• Make relevant and focused recommendations to initiate management action

Assessment context

Budget flexing, calculation and discussion of resulting variances and actions that should be taken will be a key part of the assessment.

Qualification context

Budget flexing and variances are only tested in this unit but could appear in the synoptic assessment at Level 4.

Business context

A core part of any business is to determine its objectives and come up with a plan of how to achieve these objectives (strategy). Budgeting provides detail of how the business should operate in order to achieve its objectives. A business must then monitor how it is performing against its budget and take actions to ensure its performance is as strong as possible.

Chapter overview

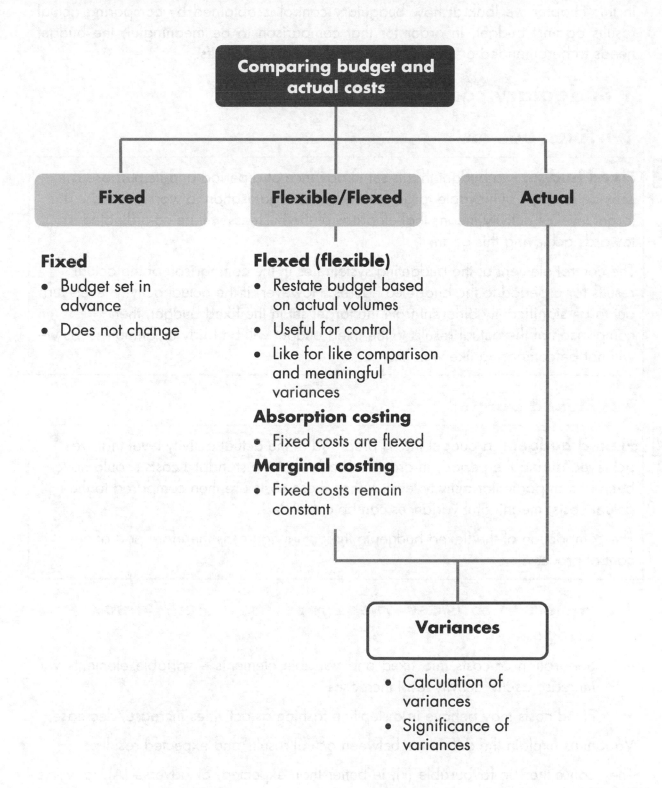

Comparing budget and actual costs

Fixed

Flexible/Flexed

Actual

Fixed
- Budget set in advance
- Does not change

Flexed (flexible)
- Restate budget based on actual volumes
- Useful for control
- Like for like comparison and meaningful variances

Absorption costing
- Fixed costs are flexed

Marginal costing
- Fixed costs remain constant

Variances

- Calculation of variances
- Significance of variances

Introduction

In this chapter we look at how budgetary control is obtained by comparing actual results against budget. In order for that comparison to be meaningful, the budget needs to be amended or 'flexed' in line with the actual results.

1 Budgetary control

1.1 Fixed budget

Key term

Fixed budget – a budget that is set in advance of a period and its purpose is to provide a single achievable target for the entire organisation to work towards. This target level of activity means that all areas of the business will be co-ordinated towards achieving this goal.

The control element of the budgeting system lies in the comparison of the actual results for a period to the budgeted figures. However, if the actual activity levels turn out to be significantly different from the target set in the fixed budget, then comparison of the actual results to the fixed budget will be fairly meaningless, as we will not be comparing like with like.

1.2 Flexed budget

Key term

Flexed budget – a budget that is prepared at the actual activity level that was achieved during the period, in order to show what the standard costs should have been at that particular activity level. When these costs are then compared to the actual costs, meaningful variances can be calculated.

The comparison of the flexed budget to the actual figures is therefore part of the control process.

1.3 Factors to consider when preparing flexed/flexible budgets

- Separation of costs into fixed and variable elements – variable elements will increase as the activity level increases

- Fixed costs may behave in a step-line fashion as activities increase/decrease.

Variances explain the difference between actual results and expected results.

They can either be favourable (F), ie better than expected, or adverse (A), ie worse than expected.

Each standard cost is made up of a quantity element and an expenditure element. Differences in quantities are known as efficiency, usage or volume variances. Differences in expenditure are known as rate, price or expenditure variances.

Illustration 1: Fixed vs flexed budget

Martin Engineering prepares detailed budgets for each quarter of the year. The budget for Quarter 4 of 20X0 was set as follows:

Sales volume 1,000 units	Quarter 4 budget
	£
Sales revenue	40,000
Materials	(10,000)
Labour	(12,000)
Production overhead	(3,000)
Gross profit	15,000
General expenses	(8,000)
Operating profit	7,000

This budget was set on the basis of both production and sales of 1,000 units and no opening or closing inventories.

It is now the first week in January in 20X1 and the actual results for Quarter 4 are being compared to the budget:

Original budget 1,000	Sales volume (units)	Actual 1,200
£		£
40,000	Sales revenue	45,600
(10,000)	Materials	(12,480)
(12,000)	Labour	(13,800)
(3,000)	Production overhead	(3,200)
15,000	Gross profit	16,120
(8,000)	General expenses	(9,080)
7,000	Operating profit	7,040

Variance report

Original budget 1,000	Sales volume (units)	Actual 1,200	Variance
£		£	£
40,000	Sales revenue	45,600	5,600 Fav
(10,000)	Materials	(12,480)	2,480 Adv
(12,000)	Labour	(13,800)	1,800 Adv
(3,000)	Production overhead	(3,200)	200 Adv
15,000	Gross profit	16,120	1,120 Fav
(8,000)	General expenses	(9,080)	1,080 Adv
7,000	Operating profit	7,040	40 Fav

It would appear that there is a mixture of variances, with favourable variances for sales and profit, but adverse variances for all of the costs.

The problem, however, is that the budget and the actual figures are not strictly comparable. The budget was based upon sales and production of 1,000 units, whereas the **actual** activity level was 1,200 units of sales and production.

We will now flex the budget to the actual activity level of 1,200 units.

Sales

Budgeted selling price	=	£40,000/1,000 units
	=	£40 per unit

The details of the cost behaviour of each of the costs are given below:

Materials	The materials cost is totally variable
Labour	Each employee can only produce 250 units each quarter – the cost of each employee is £3,000 each quarter
Production overhead	The production overhead is a totally fixed cost
General expenses	The general expenses are made up of a budgeted fixed cost of £5,000 and a variable element

Therefore, the budgeted sales revenue for 1,200 units is:

Sales	=	1,200 × £40
	=	£48,000

Materials are totally variable

Budgeted materials per unit	=	£10,000/1,000 units
	=	£10 per unit
Budgeted materials cost for 1,200 units	=	1,200 × £10
	=	£12,000

Labour is a stepped cost.

One employee is required for every 250 units, therefore for 1,200 units, five employees will be required.

Budgeted labour cost	=	5 × £3,000
	=	£15,000

Production overheads is a fixed cost so remains unchanged.

Budgeted cost for 1,200 units	=	£3,000

General expenses are a semi-variable cost.

		£
At 1,000 units	Fixed element	=	5,000
	Variable element	=	3,000
	Total		8,000

Variable element = £3,000/1,000 units = £3 per unit

			£
At 1,200 units	Fixed element	=	5,000
	Variable element		
	1,200 × £3	=	3,600
			8,600

The flexed budget will appear as follows:

Sales volume 1,200 units	Quarter 4 flexed budget
	£
Sales revenue	48,000
Materials	(12,000)
Labour	(15,000)
Production overhead	(3,000)
Gross profit	18,000
General expenses	(8,600)
Operating profit	9,400

The flexed budget can then be compared with the actual figures in the form of an operating statement, and the true variances calculated.

Martin Engineering: Quarter 4 Operating Statement

Original budget 1,000 £	Sales volume (units)	Flexed Budget 1,200 £	Actual 1,200 £	Variance £
40,000	Sales revenue	48,000	45,600	2,400 Adv
(10,000)	Materials	(12,000)	(12,480)	480 Adv
(12,000)	Labour	(15,000)	(13,800)	1,200 Fav
(3,000)	Production overhead	(3,000)	(3,200)	200 Adv
15,000	Gross profit	18,000	16,120	1,880 Adv
(8,000)	General expenses	(8,600)	(9,080)	480 Adv
7,000	Operating profit	9,400	7,040	2,360 Adv

We can now see that there is a significant adverse profit variance, with all the variances other than labour being adverse.

Activity 1: Flexed budget 1

The budget for production supervisors' costs for a period for a business at an activity level of 120,000 units is £12,000. One production supervisor is required for every 50,000 units of production.

Required

If actual production is 180,000 units, what figure would appear in the flexed budget for production supervisors' costs?

£ [   ]

1.4 Limitations of budget flexing

Although it is useful to flex budgets to eliminate volume related variances, you must bear in mind that the flexed budget is still indirectly based on the assumptions applied when the original budget was drawn up.

These assumptions may not always hold true at flexed volumes and the budget assumptions may need to be revisited when assessing performance against a flexed budget.

Budget flexing, therefore, is not a means of rebudgeting for a new strategy, since this means the underlying assumptions, other than volume, will change.

Problems with budget flexing include the following:

- Splitting mixed costs is not always straightforward.

- Fixed costs may behave in a step-line fashion as activity levels increase/decrease.

- Consideration must be given to the assumptions upon which the original fixed budget was based. Such assumptions might include the constraint posed by limiting factors, the rate of inflation, judgements about future uncertainty, or demand for the organisation's products.

- By flexing a budget, a manager is effectively saying, 'If I knew then what I know now, this is the budget I would have set'. It is a useful concept but can lead to some concern as managers can become confused and frustrated if faced with continually moving targets.

1.5 Variable or semi-variable cost?

In some instances in assessments, you may not be specifically told whether costs are variable, semi-variable or fixed. Instead you may be given budgets at different levels of activity and from these, you must determine whether the costs are variable or semi-variable.

Activity 2: Flexed budget 2

Given below is the manufacturing cost budget for Katt Ltd at two different activity levels.

	10,000 units	15,000 units
	£	£
Materials cost	12,000	18,000
Labour cost	13,000	15,750
Production overhead	4,000	4,000

Required

You are to determine the cost behaviour of each individual cost and then to determine the cost budget at an activity level of 12,000 units.

Materials

Cost per unit @ 10,000 units   =

Cost per unit @ 15,000 units   =

Materials cost @ 12,000 units   =

Labour

Cost per unit @ 10,000 units   =

Cost per unit @ 15,000 units   =

Variable element

	Activity level	Cost
		£
Level 1	10,000	
Level 2	15,000	
Increase	5,000	
Variable element	=	

Fixed element

	£
Cost @ 10,000 units	
Variable element	
Fixed element (bal fig)	
Total cost	

The labour cost at an activity level of 12,000 units:

	£
Variable element	
Fixed element	
Total cost	

Production overhead

Manufacturing cost budget @ 12,000 units

	£
Materials cost	
Labour cost	
Production overhead	

Activity 3: Flexed budget 3

The budgeted production overhead for a business is £15,800 at an activity level of 2,000 units, and £19,950 at an activity level of 3,000 units.

Required

If the actual activity level is 2,600 units, what is the flexed budget figure for production overhead?

£ [   ]

2 Comparing actual results to budgeted figures

It is important to ensure that you prepare any budget in an appropriate format. This may be according to absorption costing principles or marginal costing principles, depending upon the policy of your organisation.

What is equally important is that the actual results are reported in the same manner as the budget, in order to ensure that any variances are meaningful.

Therefore, if the budget is set under marginal costing principles, the actual results that are compared to the budget must also be recorded under marginal costing principles.

2.1 Variance proformas

2.1.1 Material variances

The direct material total variance can be subdivided into the direct material price variance and the direct material usage variance.

The direct material total variance is the difference between what the output actually cost and what it should have cost, in terms of material.

The direct material price variance is the difference between the standard cost and the actual cost for the actual quantity of material used or purchased. In other words, it is the difference between what the material did cost and what it should have cost.

The direct material usage variance is the difference between the standard quantity of materials that should have been used for the number of units actually produced, and the actual quantity of materials used, valued at the standard cost per unit of material. In other words, it is the difference between how much material should have been used and how much material was used, valued at standard cost.

		£
Total		
'Should'	Actual output (should cost)	X
'Did'	Actual output (did cost)	(X)
		X
Price		
'Should'	Actual purchases (should cost)	(X)
'Did'	Actual purchases (did cost)	X
		Kg
Usage		X
'Should'	Actual production (should use)	(X)
'Did'	Actual production (did use)	X
	Difference valued at standard cost	£X

2.1.2 Labour variances

The direct labour total variance can be subdivided into the **direct labour rate** variance and the **direct labour efficiency** variance.

The **direct labour total variance** is the difference between what the output should have cost and what it did cost, in terms of labour.

The **direct labour rate variance** is the difference between the standard cost and the actual cost for the actual number of hours paid for. In other words, it is the difference between what the labour did cost and what it should have cost.

The **direct labour efficiency variance** is the difference between the hours that should have been worked for the number of units actually produced, and the actual number of hours worked, valued at the standard rate per hour.

Total

		£
'Should'	Actual output (should cost)	X
'Did'	Actual output (did cost)	(X)
		X

Rate

		£
'Should'	Actual hours (should cost)	X
'Did'	Actual hours paid (did cost)	(X)
		X

Efficiency

		Hrs
'Should'	Actual production (should take)	X
'Did'	Actual production (did take)	(X)
	Difference valued at standard rate per hour	X
		£X

Idle time

		Hrs
'Should'	Hours worked	X
'Did'	Hours paid	(X)
	Difference valued at standard rate per hour	£X

2.1.3 Variable overhead variances

Expenditure

		£
'Should'	Actual hours worked (should cost)	X
'Did'	Actual hours worked (did cost)	(X)
		X

Efficiency

		Hrs
'Should'	Actual production (should take)	X
'Did'	Actual production (did take)	(X)
	Difference valued at standard rate per hour	X
		£X

Note. This assumes variable overheads are incurred per labour hour.

2.1.4 Fixed overhead variances

Under **marginal costing**, the fixed overhead variance is just the difference between budgeted and actual fixed overhead costs, ie fixed overhead expenditure variance.

Under **absorption costing**, the fixed overhead variance can be further subdivided as follows:

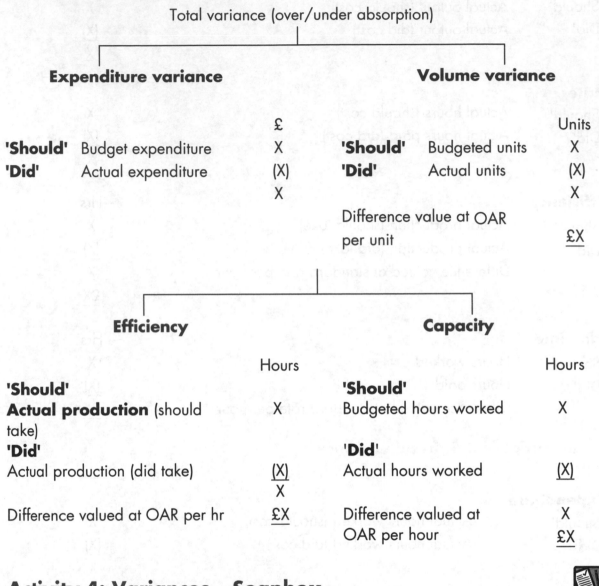

Total variance (over/under absorption)

Expenditure variance

		£
'Should'	Budget expenditure	X
'Did'	Actual expenditure	(X)
		X

Volume variance

		Units
'Should'	Budgeted units	X
'Did'	Actual units	(X)
		X
Difference value at OAR per unit		£X

Efficiency

	Hours
'Should'	
Actual production (should take)	X
'Did'	
Actual production (did take)	(X)
	X
Difference valued at OAR per hr	£X

Capacity

	Hours
'Should'	
Budgeted hours worked	X
'Did'	
Actual hours worked	(X)
Difference valued at OAR per hour	X
	£X

Activity 4: Variances – Soapbox

SoapBox produces soap and shampoo. It has several divisions, including the shampoo division which produces a concentrated shampoo that it packages in plastic bottles.

The shampoo division operates a standard cost system and the standard cost for a bottle of concentrated shampoo is as follows:

	£
Liquid shampoo – 0.25 litres @£6 per litre	1.50
Plastic bottle	0.20
Direct labour – 0.03 hours @ £11 per hour	0.33
Fixed overheads	0.70
Total cost	2.73

Actual results for May 20X9 are as follows:

11,000 bottles were produced using:

	£
2,800 litres of liquid shampoo	15,400
11,300 plastic bottles	2,034
350 direct labour hours	3,325

Total fixed overheads amounted to £7,500.

(a) **You are required to calculate the following variances for May 20X9. For each variance, state if it is favourable or adverse.**

   (i) **Direct material price variance for plastic bottles**

   (ii) **Direct material usage variance for plastic bottles**

   (iii) **Direct material price variance for liquid shampoo**

   (iv) **Direct material usage variance for liquid shampoo**

   (v) **Direct labour rate variance**

   (vi) **Direct labour efficiency variance, assuming 10,000 bottles were budgeted to produced**

   (vii) **Fixed overhead expenditure variance**

   (viii) **Fixed overhead volume variance**

(b) **Using the variances you have calculated, prepare an operating statement for May which reconciles the standard cost of total actual production with the actual cost of total actual production.**

The production director has reviewed the variances and given you the following information:

- The shampoo was of lower quality and this resulted in the machines needing to be cleaned more frequently.

- A machine broke down because it became blocked with shampoo, resulting in damage to the bottles and unproductive labour time.

(c) **Using the information provided by the production director, draft an email for the finance director explaining possible reasons for the following variances:**

   (i) **Direct material shampoo price**

   (ii) **Direct material shampoo usage**

   (iii) **Direct labour rate**

   (vi) **Direct labour efficiency**

(a)

(b) **Operating statement for May 20X9**

			£
Budgeted/standard cost for actual			
Variances	*Favourable*	*Adverse*	
Direct material price plastic bottles			
Direct material usage plastic bottles			
Direct material price liquid shampoo			
Direct material usage liquid shampoo			
Direct labour rate			
Direct labour efficiency			
Fixed overhead expenditure			
Fixed overhead volume			
Total variance			
Actual cost of actual production			

(c)

Email	
To: Finance Director	From: Accounting Technician
Subject: Variances	Date: xx/xx/xxxx

Note. Enter adverse variances as negative numbers when instructed to do so.

Activity 5: Variances – QuikMaid Ltd

QuikMaid Ltd is a specialist retailer that sells a blender machine.

The following is a copy of the original budget and the actual performance of the company's current financial year. The original budget is based on the forecast level of sales achieved at the end of the company's last financial year.

Draft budget and actual results

	Budget		Actual	
Sales volume (units)	400,000		500,000	
Production volume (units)	400,000		502,000	
	£000	£000	£000	£000
Turnover		14,000		20,000
Purchases	4,800		6,500	
Wages	2,600		3,350	
Warehousing costs	720		800	
Distribution costs	60		90	
Insurance	12		10	
Rent and rates	15		18	
Other administration	28		33	
Depreciation	50		50	
Total expenses		8,285		10,851
Less closing stock		–		40
Cost of sales		8,285		10,811
Operating profit		5,715		9,189

Warehousing costs are semi-variable.

- The budgeted fixed cost for warehousing is £40,000.
- The actual fixed cost for warehousing was £50,000.

Assumptions made when preparing the original budget

- There were no opening or closing stocks.
- Distribution cost is a stepped cost, varying with every 100,000 blenders sold.
- Insurance is considered a fixed cost.
- There were no purchases or sales of fixed assets during the year.

Required

(a) Calculate the following budgeted data:

    (i)   Selling price per unit
    (ii) Cost of purchases per unit
    (iii) Variable cost of wages per unit
    (iv) Variable cost of warehousing per unit
    (v) Distribution costs per 100,000 blenders.

(b) Calculate the following actual data:

   (i) Selling price per unit

   (ii) Cost of purchases per unit

   (iii) Variable cost of wages per unit

   (iv) Variable cost of warehousing per unit

   (v) Distribution costs per 100,000 blenders.

(c) Prepare a marginal (or variable) cost operating statement to show:

   (i) A flexed budget for the actual turnover of 500,000 units

   (ii) The budgeted and actual marginal costs associated with that turnover

   (iii) The budgeted and actual contribution

   (iv) The budgeted and actual operating profit

   (v) Any resulting variances (in £ and %) between the budgeted and actual results for the company's last financial year.

(a) Budget data:

   (i) Selling price per unit   ☐

   (ii) Cost of purchases per unit   ☐

   (iii) Variable cost of wages per unit   ☐

   (iv) Variable cost of warehousing per unit   ☐

   (v) Distribution costs per 100,000 blenders   ☐

(b)   Actual data:

(i)   Selling price per unit

☐

(ii)   Cost of purchases per unit

☐

(iii)   Variable cost of wages per unit

☐

(iv)   Variable cost of warehousing per unit

☐

(v)   Distribution costs per 100,000 blenders

☐

(c) Marginal cost operating statement:

	Budget		Actual		Variance	
Sales volume						
Production volume						
	£000	£000	£000	£000	£000	%
Turnover						
Variable costs						
Purchases						
Wages						
Warehousing costs						
Total variable costs						
Contribution						
Fixed costs						
Warehousing costs						
Distribution costs						
Insurance						
Rent and rates						
Other administration						
Depreciation						
Total fixed costs						
Operating profit						

3 The significance of budget variances

By comparing the flexed budget with the actual results, we can calculate variances. However, these variances must then be investigated and reasons for them found, so that we can determine whether actions must be taken to improve the performance of the business.

The variances can reveal significant information about the performance of the business. Management need to be informed of any significant issues that arise so that appropriate action can be taken.

Variances can reveal changes that need to be made to the planning assumptions and budgets, operational issues, and issues with motivation and accountability.

The cause of the variance must be determined before appropriate action can be taken. An employee should only be judged on what they have control over.

(a) Different **controllable** expenditure
(b) Different **uncontrollable** expenditure
(c) Inaccurate standard due to:

- Poor planning
- Use of unrealistic standards or out of date standards.

Management action may include:

(a) Correcting poor performance
(b) Encouraging good performance
(c) Updating the standard/budget

3.1 When to investigate

It may not be appropriate to investigate all variances. Before deciding whether to investigate a variance, a manager should consider:

(a) **Size of variance** – only variances that are material (ie significant to the operations and results of the organisation) will need to be investigated. The materiality level will be set by, usually as an amount in £ or a percentage of the standard cost.

(b) **Controllability of variance** – managers can only be responsible for variances within their control. Example of variances outside control are: adverse production overhead variances due to an unexpected increase in factory rent by landlord; general expenses variances for a division caused by head office costs allocated to all divisions.

(c) **Cost of investigation** – ie the cost vs benefit of investigating variances.

(d) **Interdependence of variances** – for example, the use of a lower grade of labour on a job than budgeted, leading to a favourable labour variance (as the labour rate is lower) but adverse materials variance, as the less skilled labour may cause more materials to be used.

(e) **Trend emerging** – some variances that are not material individually, but recur in each period, might indicate a control issue that needs to be investigated.

3.2 Reasons for variances

> **Assessment focus point**
>
> If we examine a variance calculated using a flexed budget (which will usually be the case), then the variance cannot be explained by the fact that the volume of production or sales was different from the budgeted volume.

Let's look at the specific types of variance in turn, and consider some possible reasons.

3.2.1 Materials variance

The total cost of material in a period depends on both:

- The price of the material per kg or per litre etc, and also
- The usage of the material per unit.

Therefore, you should consider both when examining a materials variance.

Adverse materials variance – price factors

- An unexpected price increase from a supplier

- Loss of a previous trade or bulk buying discount from a supplier

- Purchase of a higher grade of materials

- A deterioration in the sterling exchange rate where goods are bought from another country

Adverse materials variance – usage factors

- Greater wastage due to a lower grade of material
- Greater wastage due to use of a lower grade of labour
- Problems with machinery

Favourable materials variance – price factors

- Negotiation of a better price from a supplier

- Negotiation of a trade or bulk purchase discount from a supplier

- Purchase of a lower grade of materials

- An improvement in the sterling exchange rate when goods are bought from another country

Favourable materials variance – usage factors

- Use of a higher grade of material which led to less wastage
- Use of more skilled labour leading to less wastage than normal
- New machinery which provides greater efficiency

3.2.2 Labour variance

The total cost of labour in a period depends on both:

- The labour rate per hour
- The labour hours per unit

Therefore, you should consider both when examining a labour variance.

Adverse labour variance – rate factors

- Unexpected increase in the rates of pay for employees
- Use of a higher grade of labour than anticipated
- Unexpectedly high levels of overtime

Adverse labour variance – hours factors

- Use of a less skilled grade of labour
- Use of a lower grade of material which takes longer to work on
- More idle time than budgeted
- Poor supervision of the workforce
- Problems with machinery

Favourable labour variance – rate factors

- Use of a lower grade of labour than budgeted for
- Less overtime than budgeted for

Favourable labour variance – hours factors

- Use of a more skilled grade of labour
- Use of a higher grade of material which takes less time to work on
- Less idle time than budgeted
- Use of new more efficient machinery

3.2.3 Overhead variance – adverse or favourable

Be sure to comment on the variances relating to fixed overheads as well as variable production costs.

For example, investment in a new machine which may lead to material and labour variances may also lead to increased power costs, and increased depreciation. Alternatively, the costs of materials maintenance may decrease.

Other common cost variances surround salaries of directors and office staff. For example, an adverse marketing overheads variance may be caused by the employment of a new sales and marketing director with a higher salary than expected. However, this may also have an impact on the sales of the business, if the director implemented a change in sales price, ie an increase in price would lead to a favourable sales price variance. Note that the influence of the sales and marketing director may be such that sales volume may increase, but remember that a favourable sales variance cannot be due to an increased volume of sales, as the flexed budget already reflects this increase.

Assessment focus point

When asked to give possible reasons for variances in a task, do not just repeat the lists given in this chapter. Instead, you should refer to information that you are given in the task, which will flag up possible reasons for you.

Illustration 2: Explanation of variances and recommended action

Given below is an extract from the operating statement for Lawson Ltd. The budget has already been flexed to reflect actual levels of production and sales.

Operating statement – July

	Budget £	Actual £	Variance £
Materials	48,800	47,600	1,200
Labour	55,800	58,400	(2,600)
Fixed overheads	62,000	57,000	5,000

Upon investigation of the variances, the following is discovered:

- The supplier of the materials has permanently increased its prices but has also significantly improved the quality of the material.

- Some of the workforce used in the period were of a lower grade than normal and they were not as familiar with the production process as the normal workforce.

- During the period, there was a machine breakdown which caused a significant amount of idle time when the workforce was not actually able to make the product.

- Due to the machine breakdown, the power costs for the period were lower than anticipated.

- Lawson Ltd has recently reduced the amount of factory space that it rents but the standard rental cost has not been adjusted.

An email to the operations manager, identifying possible causes of the variances and making any suggestions for action that should be taken, could be written as follows.

To: Operations Manager, Lawson Ltd
From: An Accountant
Date: 31 August 20X1
Subject: Variances

The materials, labour and fixed overhead variances for the period have been calculated.

The supplier of the materials has permanently increased its prices, which might be expected to give an adverse materials variance. However, the quality of the material has also been improved, meaning that the usage of the material has improved by more than the effect of the increased price, leading to the overall favourable materials variance.

We should consider other suppliers for the supply of our materials, but if their prices are the same as our supplier's, or the material quality is not as good, then the standard cost of the materials should be altered. If it can be shown that the higher quality material has caused the favourable variance through reduced usage then consideration should also be given to alteration of the standard materials usage per unit ie to budgeted material costs in future periods.

A favourable labour variance may have been expected due to the use of lower grade labour than normal for some of the period, but the adverse labour variance suggests that the lower grade labour may be less efficient than the previous labour ie take longer to perform the same tasks. These inefficiencies have overridden any benefit of the lower labour rate. Labour inefficiencies (and so an adverse labour variance) may also have been caused by the machine breakdown during the period, which meant that labour hours were paid for when no productive work was achieved (idle time).

The machine breakdown is a one-off event which should not be built into the budgeted costs for subsequent periods. However, if it is anticipated that the lower grade of labour will now normally be used for production, then the standard labour rate and hours should be changed.

The fixed overhead variance was favourable due to lower power costs, the machine breakdown and also the reduction in factory rental. This is despite any additional costs of repair which may have been incurred because of the breakdown (and which would have been expected to lead to an adverse variance). The reduction in rent is a permanent reduction and therefore the budgeted fixed overhead should be altered to reflect this in future periods.

Activity 6: Explaining variances – QuikMaid

The operating statement for QuikMaid's current financial year is shown below:

	Budget		Actual		Variance	
Sales volume	500,000		500,000			
Production volume	500,000		500,000			
	£000	£000	£000	£000	£000	%
Turnover		17,500		20,000	2,500 F	14.3
Variable costs						
Purchases (500,000 × £12)	6,000		6,475		475 A	7.9
Wages (500,000 × £6.50)	3,250		3,335		85 A	2.6
Warehousing costs (500,000 × £1.70)	850		745		105 F	12.4
		10,100		10,555	455 A	4.5
Contribution		7,400		9,445	2,045 F	27.6
Fixed Costs						
Warehousing costs	40		50		10 A	25.0
Distribution costs	75		90		15 A	20.0
Insurance	12		10		2 F	16.7
Rent and rates	15		18		3 A	20.0
Other administration	28		33		5 A	17.9
Depreciation	50		50		–	–
		220		251	31 A	14.1
Operating profit		7,180		9,194	2,014 F	28.1

Required

Write an email that gives an analysis of the actual results. This email should:

(a) Analyse the significance of EACH of the variances and explain how EACH could have arisen.

(b) Explain TWO procedures that could be introduced in order to achieve a better sales budget forecast.

(c) Explain THREE steps that Quikmaid Ltd can take to motivate managers to achieve budgets.

```
┌─────────────────────────────────────────────────────────────────┐
│                            Email                                  │
│  To: XXXX                              From: Accounting Technician │
│  Subject: Analysis of results          Date:  xx/xx/xxxx          │
├─────────────────────────────────────────────────────────────────┤
│  (a)  Significance of and reason for the variances                │
│                                                                   │
│                                                                   │
│                                                                   │
│                                                                   │
│                                                                   │
│  (b)  Two procedures that could lead to a better sales budget     │
│                                                                   │
│                                                                   │
│                                                                   │
│                                                                   │
│  (c)  Three steps that could motivate managers                    │
│                                                                   │
│                                                                   │
│                                                                   │
│                                                                   │
│                                                                   │
└─────────────────────────────────────────────────────────────────┘
```

Chapter summary

- A fixed budget is set in advance of a budgeting period as a pre-determined plan of activity for all areas of a business.

- A flexed budget can be prepared which adjusts the budget to reflect the actual activity level or volume for the period.

- A flexed budget is used in the control aspect of the budgetary system as the actual results are compared to the flexed budget in order to determine any variances.

- In order to flex a budget, a distinction must be drawn between variable costs and fixed costs, and the variable or fixed elements of a semi-variable cost – the variable elements of cost will increase or decrease with changes in activity level, whereas the fixed elements of cost do not vary with changes in activity levels.

- Budgets and actual results may be reported, either using absorption or marginal costing techniques.

- Fixed overhead absorption rates and budgeted activity levels can be used to calculate budgeted fixed overheads for use in a flexed budget.

- Each type of variance can have a variety of causes – often the variances are interdependent, meaning that one factor which caused one variance is also the factor that caused other variances.

- Consideration must be given to whether or not variances should be investigated – considerations include the materiality (significance) of the variance, the trend of variances and the controllability of costs.

Keywords

- **Controllable variances:** variances over which the manager of a responsibility centre has influence

- **Fixed budget:** a budget set in advance of a period in order to act as a plan of action for the whole organisation

- **Flexed budget:** a budget prepared for the actual activity level for the period

- **Interdependence of variances:** this is where the factor which causes one variance can also be the cause of another variance

Activity answers

Activity 1: Flexed budget 1

The correct answer is:

£ | 16,000

Working

At 120,000 units – 3 supervisors required – cost	=£12,000/3
	=£4,000 each
At 180,000 units – 4 supervisors required – cost	=£16,000

Activity 2: Flexed budget 2

Materials

Cost per unit @ 10,000 units	=	£12,000/10,000
	=	£1.20
Cost per unit @ 15,000 units	=	£18,000/15,000
	=	£1.20

This is, therefore, a purely variable cost.

Materials cost @ 12,000 units	=	12,000 × £1.20
	=	£14,400

Labour

Cost per unit @ 10,000 units	=	£13,000/10,000
	=	£1.30
Cost per unit @ 15,000 units	=	£15,750/15,000
	=	£1.05

Therefore, this is not a purely variable cost but it is also clearly not fixed. We will have to assume that it is a semi-variable cost and apply the high low method using the costs at the two activity levels to determine the fixed and variable element.

	Activity level	Cost £
Level 1	10,000	13,000
Level 2	15,000	15,750
Increase	5,000	2,750

Variable element	=	£2,750/5,000 units
	=	£0.55 per unit

Fixed element:

	£
Cost @ 10,000 units	
Variable element 10,000 × £0.55	5,500
Fixed element (bal fig)	7,500
Total cost	13,000

The labour cost at an activity level of 12,000 units will therefore be:

	£
Variable element 12,000 units × £0.55	6,600
Fixed element	7,500
Total cost	14,100

Production overhead

As this is the same cost at 10,000 units and 15,000 units, the production overhead can be assumed to be a fixed cost (marginal costing principles have been used).

Manufacturing cost budget @ 12,000 units

	£
Materials cost	14,400
Labour cost	14,100
Production overhead	4,000

Activity 3: Flexed budget 3

The correct answer is:

£	18,290

Working

Cost per unit at 2,000 units = £15,800/2,000

= £7.90

Cost per unit at 3,000 units = £19,950/3,000

= £6.65

Therefore, this is a semi-variable cost.

	Activity level	**Cost**
	Units	£
	2,000	15,800
	3,000	19,950
Increase	1,000	4,150
Variable element	=	£4,150/1,000
	=	£4.15 per unit

	£
At 2,000 units:	
Variable element 2,000 units × £4.15	8,300
Fixed element (bal fig)	7,500
Total cost	15,800
At 2,600 units:	
Variable element 2,600 units × £4.15	10,790
Fixed element	7,500
Total cost	18,290

Activity 4: Variances - Soapbox

(a)   Variance calculations

    (i)   **Direct material price variance for plastic bottles**

		£
'Should'	11,300 bottles should cost @£0.20	2,260
'Did'	Actual purchases did cost	(2,034)
		226 F

    (ii)   **Direct material usage variance for plastic bottles**

Usage		Bottles
'Should'	11,000 units should use @ 1 bottle	11,000
'Did'	Actual production did use	(11,300)
	Difference valued at standard cost £0.20	300
		£60 A

    (iii)   **Direct material price variance for liquid shampoo**

		£
'Should'	2,800 litres should cost @£6	16,800
'Did'	Actual purchases did cost	(15,400)
		1,400 F

    (iv)   **Direct material usage variance for liquid shampoo**

Usage		Litres
'Should'	11,000 units should use @ 0.25 litres	2,750
'Did'	Actual production did use	(2,800)
	Difference valued at standard cost £6	50
		£300 A

(v) Direct labour rate variance

		£
'Should'	350 hours should cost @£11	3,850
'Did'	Actual hours did cost	(3,325)
		525 F

(vi) Direct labour efficiency variance

Efficiency

		Hours
'Should'	11,000 units should use @ 0.03 hours	330
'Did'	Actual production did use	(350)
	Difference valued at standard cost £11	20
		£220 A

(vii) Fixed overhead expenditure variance

		£
'Should'	Budget expenditure	7,000
'Did'	Actual expenditure	(7,500)
		500 A

(viii) Fixed overhead volume variance

		Units
'Should'	Budgeted units	10,000
'Did'	Actual units	(11,000)
		1,000
Difference value at OAR per unit £0.70		£700 F

(b) Operating statement

	Favourable £	Adverse £	£
Budgeted/standard cost for actual (11,000 × £2.73)			30,030
Variances			
Direct material price plastic bottles	226		
Direct material usage plastic bottles		60	
Direct material price liquid shampoo	1,400		
Direct material usage liquid shampoo		300	
Direct labour rate	525		
Direct labour efficiency		220	
Fixed overhead expenditure		500	
Fixed overhead volume	700		
Total variance	2,851	1,080	1,771F
Actual cost of actual production			28,259

(c)   Email

> ### (i)   Direct materials (shampoo) price variance
>
> The direct shampoo price variance is £1,400 favourable. This appears to be due to the purchase of lower quality shampoo which has resulted in the adverse usage variance of £300.
>
> ### (ii)   Direct materials (shampoo) usage variance
>
> The direct materials usage variance was £300 adverse, which may be due to the low quality material causing the machine to break down and waste material.
>
> ### (iii)   Direct labour rate variance
>
> The direct labour rate variance was £525 favourable meaning that a lower rate was paid than expected. This may have been due to a lower skilled level of labour.
>
> ### (iv)   Direct labour efficiency variance
>
> The direct labour efficiency variance was £220 adverse. This may be due to the poor quality of the materials or it may have been due to a lower skilled labour force.

Activity 5: Variances – Quikmaid Ltd

(a)   Calculation of budgeted data

(i)   Budgeted selling price per unit   £14,000,000/400,000 = £35

(ii)   Budgeted cost of purchases per unit   £4,800,000/400,000 = £12

(iii)   Budgeted variable cost of wages per unit   £2,600,000/400,000 = £6.50

(iv)   Budgeted variable cost of warehousing

Total cost   £720,000

Less fixed cost $\dfrac{£40,000}{£680,000}$

$\dfrac{£680,000}{£400,000}$ = £1.70

(v)   Budgeted distribution costs per 100,000 blenders

£60,000/(400,000/100,000) = £15,000

(b)   Calculation of actual data

(i)   Actual selling price per unit   £20,000,000/500,000 = £40

(ii)   Actual cost of purchases per unit £6,500,000/502,000 = £12.95

(iii)   Actual variable cost of wages per unit £3,350,000/502,000 = £6.67

(iv) Actual variable cost of warehousing

Total cost £800,000

Less fixed cost $\dfrac{£50,000}{£750,000}$

$\dfrac{£750,000}{£502,000} = £1.49$

(v) Actual distribution costs per 100,000 blenders

£90,000/(500,000/100,000) = £18,000

(c)

	Budget		Actual		Variance	
Sales volume	500,000		500,000			
Production volume	500,000		500,000			
	£000	£000	£000	£000	£000	%
Turnover		17,500		20,000	2,500 F	14.3
Variable costs						
Purchases (500,000 × £12)	6,000		6,475		475 A	7.9
Wages (500,000 × £6.50)	3,250		3,335 (W1)		85 A	2.6
Warehousing costs (500,000 × £1.70)	850		745 (W2)		105 F	12.4
		10,100		10,555	455 A	4.5
Contribution		7,400		9,445	2,045 F	27.6
Fixed Costs						
Warehousing costs	40		50		10 A	25.0
Distribution costs	75		90		15 A	20.0
Insurance	12		10		2 F	16.7
Rent and rates	15		18		3 A	20.0
Other administration	28		33		5 A	17.9
Depreciation	50		50		–	–
		220		251	31 A	14.1
Operating profit		7,180		9,194	2,014 F	28.1

(W1) 500,000 × £6.67 = £3,335,000

(W2) 500,000 × £1.49 = £745,000

Activity 6: Explaining variances – QuikMaid

Email

To:	XXXXX
From:	Accountant
Subject:	Analysis of results for last financial year
Date:	XX/XX/XXXX

(a) Significance of each of the variances and how they arose

The actual selling price was £5 more than budgeted. The overall effect of this was to increase income and it is this that has given the overall favourable variance of £2,500,000 for the year. We were able to charge the extra price due to the increase in demand for the blender.

There is an adverse variance on materials used of £475,000. This arises from an increase in actual unit costs over the budgeted price of £0.95.

Of the other variances, the most significant are the adverse labour variance of £85,000 (but this is only 2.6% of the budgeted cost) and the favourable variance on warehousing costs of £95,000.

The direct labour unit rate has risen from £6.50 to £6.67 per unit. This could be because the increased production has resulted in more overtime hours being worked or because more skilled staff were used.

The favourable variance on warehousing reflects the unit cost decrease from £1.70 to £1.49.

The fixed costs show a favourable variance for insurance. This could be due to a number of reasons, including decreased insurance costs through a good claims record, or renegotiation of cover required.

The adverse variances on distribution (20%) rent and rates (20%) and other administrative expenses (17.9%) whilst smaller in absolute terms than the variable costs, are relatively large and need to be investigated.

(b) Two procedures to achieve a better sales budget forecast

Forecasts are part of the overall planning and control systems of the organisation. In our case, it may have been an improvement if we had done some market research to assess the demand for the blender and also to do some market testing on acceptable sales prices. From this, we may have been able to provide a number of budget forecasts based on different volumes and prices to use as monitoring tools.

It would also be more useful to prepare flexible budgets on a more regular basis than yearly, in order to pick up on the variations more quickly and therefore, be able to take appropriate actions to more accurately predict sales.

(c) **Three steps to motivate managers to achieve budgets (only three required)**

Maintaining motivated managers is an important aspect of setting and achieving budgets. To do this, managers should be involved in the planning process so that budgets are not set at unachievable levels.

Proper lines of communication should be established so that managers can be kept informed and to understand the part they have to play in achieving the budgets.

The establishment of performance targets that are challenging but achievable and lead to acceptable rewards, such as salary increases or bonuses, is another way of keeping managers motivated.

Ensuring managers are only accountable for items within their control should also increase motivation.

Test your learning

1 **Explain the difference between a fixed and a flexed budget and the purpose of each.**

2 **You are required to complete the following operating statement. Do this by flexing the budget (fill in the flexed budget numbers), calculating variances (fill in the variance numbers) and selecting whether each variance is favourable or adverse.**

The budget for a production company for the month of December and the actual results for the month are given below:

Original budget 4,000 £	Sales volume (units)	Flexed budget 3,600 £	Actual 3,600 £	Variance £	Favourable/ Adverse Fav/Adv
96,000	Sales revenue		90,000		▼
18,000	Materials		15,120		▼
27,200	Labour		25,200		▼
5,700	Production overhead		5,900		▼
45,100	Gross profit		43,780		▼
35,200	General expenses		32,880		▼
9,900	Operating profit		10,900		▼

The materials and labour costs are variable costs, the production overhead is a fixed cost and the general expenses are a semi-variable cost with a fixed element of £11,200.

Picklist:

Adverse
Favourable

3 Given below for January are the original budget figures, the flexed budget figures and the actual figures.

Original budget 24,000		Sales volume (units)	Flexed budget 28,000		Actual 30,000	
£	£		£	£	£	£
	72,000	Sales revenue		84,000		86,000
19,200		Materials	22,400		22,500	
33,000		Labour	37,000		41,200	
5,600		Production expenses	5,600		5,800	
	57,800	Production cost		65,000		69,500
	14,200	Gross profit		19,000		16,500
12,600		General expenses	14,200		14,700	
	1,600	Operating profit		4,800		1,800

Complete the following operating statement showing a flexed budget to reflect the actual level of activity for the month, and variances from that flexed budget for each figure.

Operating statement: January

	Flexed budget 30,000 units		Actual 30,000 units		Variance
	£	£	£	£	£
Sales revenue				86,000	
Materials			22,500		
Labour			41,200		
Production expenses			5,800		
Production cost				69,500	
Gross profit				16,500	
General expenses				14,700	
Operating profit				1,800	

4 Given below is the fixed budget for a period prepared under absorption costing principles. There were no opening inventories.

Sales volume 50,000 units

	£	£
Sales revenue		900,000
Materials	216,000	
Labour	324,000	
Production overhead	108,000	
Cost of production 54,000 units	648,000	
Less closing inventory 4,000 units	48,000	
Cost of sales		(600,000)
Gross profit		300,000
General expenses		(198,000)
Net profit		102,000

The materials and labour costs are variable costs. The production overhead and general expenses are fixed costs.

Complete the following redraft of the budget using marginal costing principles.

Marginal costing budget

	£	£
Sales revenue		
Materials		
Labour		
Cost of production		
Closing inventory		
Cost of sales		
Gross profit		
Fixed production overhead		
Fixed general expenses		
Net profit		

Explain the difference in budgeted profit between the two budgets.

5 A business has the following budgeted and actual figures for a period:

Budgeted output	240,000 units
Actual fixed overhead	£480,000
Fixed overhead absorption rate	£1.90 per unit

The fixed overhead variance comparing flexed and actual results is

£ [　　　　] [　　　　　　▼]

Picklist:

Adverse
Favourable

6   **What is a controllable cost? Why is it important that managerial performance is only judged on the basis of controllable variances?**

7   The following report has been prepared, relating to one product for March. This has been sent to the appropriate product manager as part of the company's monitoring procedures.

Variance report: 31 March

	Actual	Budget	Variance
Production volume (units)	9,905	10,000	95 A
Direct material (kg)	9,800	10,000	200 F
Direct material (£)	9,600	10,000	400 F
Direct labour (hours)	2,500	2,400	100 A
Direct labour (£)	8,500	8,400	100 A
Total variable costs	18,100	18,400	300 F

The product manager has complained that the report ignores the principle of flexible budgeting and is unfair.

Prepare a report addressed to the management team which comments critically on the monthly variance report. Include, as an appendix to your report, the layout of a revised monthly variance report which will be more useful to the product manager. Include row and column headings, but do not calculate the contents of the report.

Performance indicators in budgetary control

8

Learning outcomes

3.4	Recommend appropriate performance measures to support budgetary control
	• Suggest suitable physical and financial performance measures, consistent with key planning assumptions, to aid budgetary control
	• Calculate these measures for budget and for actual performance
	• Provide constructive advice to assist the achievement of targets and budgets.
4.4	**Effectively present budgetary issues to management**
	• Identify and describe important budgetary planning and control issues
	• Make relevant and focused recommendations to initiate management action

Assessment context

It is likely that suitable performance indicators for a particular scenario will need to be suggested and this could be within part of a written requirement in the assessment.

Qualification context

Performance indicators are also examined in several other Level 4 units.

Business context

A core part of any business is to determine key objectives and come up with a plan of how the business can achieve these objectives (strategy). *Management Accounting: Budgeting* provides detail of how the business should operate in order to achieve its objectives. Having prepared the budgets, key performance indicators will also be set so that performance can be evaluated and achievement of these targets can be assessed.

Chapter overview

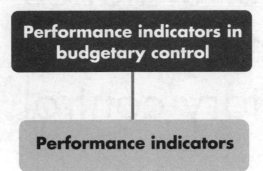

Performance indicators in budgetary control

Performance indicators

Any item can be measured. Types of measures could include indicators of:

- Quality
- Customer satisfaction
- Efficiency
- Capacity
- Cost

Introduction

In this chapter, we look at an alternative means of monitoring performance using budgets, by the setting of targets or **performance indicators**. The budgeted value of these performance measures will be consistent with the key planning assumptions of the organisation. They can then be compared against the actual values achieved by an organisation and so performance can be evaluated in this way.

1 Performance indicators in budgeting

1.1 Budgetary control

As we have seen in Chapter 7, budgetary control can be considered in the context of actual costs compared with budgeted costs, but budgetary control can also be exercised via key performance indicators.

These indicators may be financial measures but they can also be used to measure performance of non-financial targets.

1.2 Form of performance indicators

- **Absolute figures**, eg when considering materials usage, a production manager may want to know how much material (in kg) has been wasted in a day. This is an absolute number.

- **Percentage terms** eg how much material is wasted as a percentage of the total material used in production that day.

Such absolute or percentage measures are often referred to as **physical**, or **non-financial**. They are numerical, but are not expressed in £ terms.

By contrast, if the materials wastage in the day (in kg) is then multiplied by the cost per kg, this gives a **financial** measure as it is expressed in money terms ie it is the cost to the company of the material wastage in that day.

1.3 Simple financial measures

- **Average selling price per unit** – this could be compared against the retail price to give an idea of how much the price has been discounted to achieve actual volumes.

- **Profit as a percentage of sales revenue** – this could be based on gross or net profit and could be compared with other businesses to see how the organisation's percentage returns on sales compare to that of competitors.

- **Materials cost per unit of purchase** – when compared with the total unit cost, this can help management understand how much of a unit cost for a product is made up of the raw materials.

- **Labour rate per hour** – if this increases over the year by more than the average wage increases for the industry, management will probably want to know why.

- **Cost per unit of production** – as we have seen, management often want to attribute costs to cost units and monitor the movements in that cost.

In addition, as we have already seen, sales and cost variances are used to monitor performance when actual performance is compared with budgeted performance.

Assessment focus point

For Level 4 *Budgeting*, an awareness of common financial measures such as these will not be enough on its own. You need to be able to apply knowledge of how and why performance indicators of various types are constructed so that you can look at a scenario and suggest suitable measures.

It is not possible to cover every measure in this chapter. However, if you understand how performance measurement works, you should be able to identify relevant measures for any given scenario.

1.4 Comparability

As performance measures can be used in comparison with budgets or targets, it is important that we compare like with like.

Illustration 1: Comparability

Say the production manager finds out that the material wastage in a day is actually 20 kg, but the budgeted figure is 50 kg, he or she will be happy with the performance. However, if the budgeted figure actually relates to the targeted wastage over a period of five days ie 10 kg wastage per day on average, the actual performance is shown to be poor.

1.5 Areas of performance

- **Quality** – usually in relation to units of finished goods, but sometimes used when considering materials

- **Wastage of materials**

- **Efficiency and productivity** – relates to labour, but also machinery

- **Capacity** – can also relate to machinery or labour

Assessment focus point

It is important that you do not just learn the measures discussed in this chapter as a definitive list. In the assessment, you may be asked to identify suitable performance measures for a particular business or scenario which is not specifically covered here. Think carefully about the resources used by the business and this should help you identify useful measures.

Suitable performance indicators will vary, depending on whether a business is in manufacturing, retail or service, and you should consider this when asked to identify appropriate measures.

2 Quality

Suitable performance indicators for the **quality** of physical goods could be a mixture of non-financial and financial performance indicators.

Activity 1: Non-financial indicators

Required

Suggest possible non-financial measures or indicators of quality.

Activity 2: Financial indicators

Required

Suggest possible financial measures or indicators of quality.

2.1 Measuring quality of services

Measuring the quality of a service again involves measuring customer satisfaction; therefore, the first step is to ensure that the organisation knows what it is that the customer expects from the service.

Some of the performance indicators for quality of a service may be qualitative, such as surveys of customer opinion. A further method of assessing the quality of a service may be by inspection, either by an internal or an external body, such as government inspections of schools.

There can also be quantitative, although normally non-financial, performance indicators for a service, such as average waiting times for hospital operations or the percentage of train journeys that did not run on time.

Activity 3: Quality performance indicators

Required

What type of quality performance indicators might a taxi firm consider?

---

3 Wastage of materials

It will be preferable for this to be minimised but some wastage may be inevitable in a production process. A budget may set a target for the amount (or percentage) of wastage in an attempt to keep this to a low level.

Illustration 2: Wastage

Lane Engineering has the following materials wastage figures for four days of production.

	Total materials used	Materials wastage
	Kg	Kg
Day 1	3,500	50
Day 2	4,200	70
Day 3	4,800	100
Day 4	5,000	80

The targets set for materials wastage in the budget were that wastage should exceed no more than 1.5% of the materials used each day, and also that no more than 90 kg per day should be wasted in total.

The production manager can see immediately that the absolute target of 90 kg per day was exceeded on Day 3, but he also calculates the percentage wastage.

		Percentage wastage
Day 1	$\dfrac{50}{3,500}$	1.43%
Day 2	$\dfrac{70}{4,200}$	1.67%
Day 3	$\dfrac{100}{4,800}$	2.08%
Day 4	$\dfrac{80}{5,000}$	1.60%

The percentage target was exceeded not only on Day 3 but also on days 2 and 4.

The reasons for the materials wastage should be investigated, as the target is not met on three out of four days. There may be a short-term reason why the materials wastage is excessive, eg if a grade of labour with lower skills than usual is being used or if the material batch is of lower quality than usual.

However, it may be that this is the best that can be achieved, and such wastage is likely to continue. If this is the case, then the target materials wastage measure is unrealistic and should be amended.

Activity 4: Wastage

The assembly department of a toy manufacturing business carries out the activity of attaching wheels onto toy cars. Occasionally, the wheels break as they are attached, and have to be discarded.

Required

Suggest two possible performance indicators relating to the usage of wheel components by the assembly department.

4 Efficiency, productivity and capacity

Efficiency, productivity and capacity are aspects of performance which, in a manufacturing business, often relate to labour. However, the efficiency and capacity of equipment or machinery can also be monitored if machine hours, rather than labour hours, are considered.

4.1 Measuring labour performance

A simple performance measure for direct labour of a business is how many units workers manage to produce in a period, compared with the budgeted level.

There could be two reasons why labour managed to produce more units than expected in the budget:

- The employees worked harder ie they were more efficient or productive

- There were more labour hours available than expected, either through overtime or an increased number of employees ie there was increased capacity.

Alternatively, an increase in activity may be due to a mixture of both these factors. A decrease in the activity could be due to employees working less hard (lower productivity), there being fewer labour hours available (lower capacity) but also if there was idle time (workers paid but without there being work to do).

Therefore, when considering performance measures to assess labour, both productivity/efficiency and capacity may be considered.

4.2 Productivity and efficiency

The terms 'efficiency' and 'productivity' are strongly related, and may be used interchangeably.

Productivity is a measure of how hard employees are working or how productive they are being in their hours at work and is often measured in terms of units of output.

Possible performance measures relating to productivity are therefore how many units of product or service are being produced, either each hour or by each employee. These measures are shown below in an equation format to help your understanding. However, in an assessment, just stating 'productivity' when asked to give a performance measure will not answer the task. You need to say what you mean by this.

$$\text{Productivity per labour hour} = \frac{\text{Output in the period}}{\text{Hours worked in the period}}$$

$$\text{Productivity per employee} = \frac{\text{Output in the period}}{\text{No of employees working on output}}$$

Illustration 3: Productivity 1

Harris Engineering has calculated the budgeted and actual results for the month of June as follows:

	Actual	Budget
Units produced	285,000	250,000
Number of production workers	30	28
Hours worked	4,800	4,400

Two possible performance measures of productivity are:

(1) The number of units produced per labour hour

$$\text{Actual productivity} = \frac{285,000 \text{ units}}{4,800 \text{ hours}}$$

$$= 59.4 \text{ units per hour}$$

$$\text{Budgeted productivity} = \frac{250,000 \text{ units}}{4,400 \text{ hours}}$$

$$= 56.8 \text{ units per labour hour}$$

(2) Number of units produced per employee

	Actual	Budget
Productivity per employee =	$\dfrac{285,000}{30}$	$\dfrac{250,000}{28}$
=	9,500 units per employee	8,929 units per employee

In this case, the actual productivity during June is high compared to the budgeted productivity, under both measures.

An increase in productivity over budget means that more units were produced in one hour or by one employee. This will normally mean a reduction in costs, as the same number of units can be produced in fewer hours and therefore with reduced labour costs, machine costs and overheads.

If the labour cost is assumed here to be £10 per hour, the labour cost has actually increased in absolute terms from £44,000 per the budget to £48,000. If this figure had been considered alone, this may have been regarded as poor performance. However, the labour cost per unit has actually decreased from

$$\text{Budgeted} = \frac{44,000}{250,000} = £0.176$$

to

$$\text{Actual} = \frac{48,000}{285,000} = £0.168$$

and this is explained by the increased productivity.

The efficiency and productivity of machinery could be considered by replacing labour hours with machine hours. Such a performance indicator would highlight if machinery was ageing or poorly maintained, and so becoming less efficient.

Illustration 4: Productivity 2

Harris Engineering has a sales department which processes all orders for goods. A suitable performance target for the sales team might be sales orders per employee.

In June, the six members of the telephone sales team processed 1,240 orders.

$$\text{Productivity per employee} = \frac{\text{Output = Number of orders}}{\text{Number of employees}}$$

$$= \frac{1,240 \text{ orders}}{6 \text{ employees}}$$

$$= 207 \text{ orders per employee}$$

Activity 5: Productivity

An advertising company budgeted for the production of 216 advertisements in the next quarter using 26 advertising executives. The actual performance in the quarter was only 188 advertisements produced by 22 executives.

Required

What was the actual productivity of the executives (to 1 decimal place) compared with budget?

	Productivity (per executive)
Actual	
Budget	
Favourable/(Adverse) variance	

4.3 Idle time ratios

This is the difference between the actual hours that have to be paid to a worker, and the number of hours that are actually put to use in production ie hours paid versus hours worked.

The number of idle time hours can be multiplied by the labour rate (cost in £) to give a financial measure.

Alternatively, this could be calculated as a ratio of the idle hours per employee:

$$\frac{\text{Total idle hours}}{\text{Number of employees}}$$

If the actual performance is monitored, and the idle hours indicator is not zero, it may be that management take the decision to redeploy workers to other areas of the business such as the manufacture of alternative products.

Note that idle time is not caused by workers working more slowly; but by there being no work to do during this time, perhaps because of a materials shortage, a machine breakdown etc.

4.4 Capacity

We said that increased productivity or efficiency is only one of the reasons why the labour force may have produced more units in a period than budgeted ie why their activity was higher than expected.

The other reason might be if the number of labour hours was actually more than budgeted. This could be because there were more employees available in this particular department, perhaps redeployed from elsewhere in the business, or because casual, seasonal staff have been employed.

Alternatively, the increased capacity could be because overtime has been paid such that individual employees have themselves worked for more hours than budgeted in the period.

Simple performance measures relating to capacity are therefore:

- The total number of hours worked by employees in the period (or even more simply, the number of employees)
- The total number of overtime hours worked
- The number of labour hours (or overtime hours) worked per employee
- The number of hours worked by casual staff in the period

We said that efficiency and capacity measures can relate to both labour and machines. Machine capacity is a particular issue for a capital intensive operation, which might include the following in its performance measures:

- The total number of machine hours in the period
- The number of hours lost through machine breakdowns

- Number (or percentage) of machines in use per day. The percentage may be described as a machine utilisation rate, but you should always explain what you mean by a suggested measure clearly.

Activity 6: Capacity

A manufacturing organisation had a budgeted output of 288,000 units planned for a 20 day period in October. 268,000 units were, in fact, produced.

There are 10 workers, each guaranteed eight hours work a day for each of the 20 days. The budgeted output would be achieved by full use of this labour, with no overtime.

However, for two half days, the machinery used in production broke down and no units could be produced.

Required

Suggest and calculate performance measures to explain why the activity was lower than expected.

5 Service organisations

Many of the performance indicators considered in this chapter will be relevant to service industries, although they will need to be expressed slightly differently. For example, a unit might be a chargeable hour in an accountancy firm or a passenger mile for a transport provider.

Productivity will also be assessed in service organisations, for example:

Service organisation	Measure of productivity
Accountancy firm	Percentage of chargeable hours to total hours
College of education	Percentage of students passing exams to total students – pass rate
Transport company	Number of passengers transported per month

Quality of performance might be measured in the following ways:

Service organisation	Measure of quality
Accountancy firm	No. of clients that leave the firm for another firm
College of education	Students; assessments of the lecturers
Transport company	Number of delays on routes

Service organisations are sometimes used as the scenario in an assessment for a number of tasks. Use the information in the scenario and the techniques that you have learnt in this chapter to adapt performance indicators to the requirements of the organisation being considered.

Activity 7: Service organisations

Required

Suggest a possible performance measure for an events planner (who plans weddings, parties and corporate events) to monitor the quality of his or her work.

Chapter summary

- Performance indicators can be calculated to summarise quality, wastage, efficiency/productivity and capacity – some of the performance indicators will be non-financial measures and some will be financial measures.

- After the performance indicators are calculated, the actual and budgeted indicators must be compared and interpreted.

- Measuring quality often involves measuring customer satisfaction with the goods or service and measures may be non-financial eg percentage of customers who complain, or financial eg cost per customer of the customer service department.

- Productivity can be measured as units produced per hour or units produced per employee.

- Service organisations will also require performance indicators but they may be slightly different from those for manufacturing or retail organisations due to the nature of the organisation.

Keywords

- **Performance indicators:** targets for operational performance
- **Productivity:** a measure of how hard employees are working
- **Quality:** a measure of defectiveness or customer satisfaction

Activity 1: Non financial indicators

- Number of goods returned
- Percentage of number of goods returned to number of goods sold
- Number of warranty claims as a percentage of total units sold
- Number of customer complaints as a percentage of total number of sales
- Percentage of defective materials compared to total materials
- Number of anticipated defective units
- Percentage of defective units to total of units produced

Activity 2: Financial indicators

- Cost per customer of the customer service department
- Cost per customer of after-sales service
- The percentage of the sales value of returned goods to total sales value
- Unit cost of returned goods
- Unit cost of repair of returned goods
- Cost of reworking defective goods as a percentage of total production cost

Activity 3: Quality performance indicators

Quality performance indicators for a taxi firm might include:

- Percentage of taxis arriving on time compared to total taxi trips made
- Percentage of repeat customers compared to total customers
- Survey results of customer satisfaction
- Number of customer complaints

Activity 4: Wastage

Assembly department performance measures for toy cars could be:

- Number of wheels discarded per day
- Number of wheels discarded as a percentage of total wheels used
- Number of wheels discarded as percentage of toy cars made
- Cost of wheels discarded per day

Note that the performance measures involving breaking wheels might involve machine or labour hours too (eg hours lost attaching wheels which break), as these are increased if time is spent attaching a wheel that then breaks, and so another wheel has to be attached. However, only two simple performance measures were required here.

Activity 5: Productivity

	Productivity (per executive)
Actual	8.5
Budget	8.3
Favourable/(Adverse) variance	0.2 Favourable

	Budget	**Actual**
Productivity		
216/26	8.3 per executive	
188/22		8.5 per executive

Activity 6: Capacity

Possible performance measures include:

- Number of hours of idle time (and cost of this if labour rate were known)

- Number of hours worked (budget vs actual)

- Budgeted and actual units made per labour hour worked

- Number of hours of idle time = 2 × 4 (half day) × 10 (number of employees who cannot work during this time) = 80 hours

The cost of idle hours would be found by multiplying the number of hours by the labour rate.

Number of hours paid/budgeted as worked = 10 × 8 × 20 = 1,600 hours

Number of hours actually worked = 1,600 – 80 = 1,520

Therefore, budgeted productivity = 288,000/1,600 = 180 units/hour

Actual productivity based on hours actually worked = 268,000/1,520 = 176 units/hour

Therefore, the reduced activity is not only due to the machine breakdown giving rise to idle time, but because the workers also worked less efficiently.

Activity 7: Service organisations

Number of new clients obtained by referral from past clients

Number (or percentage) of clients who book events again (repeat bookings)

Value of work from repeat bookings

Number of complaints by guests at the event (feedback from guests)

Number of complaints by client about event

1 **Suggest suitable performance measures for a supermarket manager to assess the performance of the cashiers.**

2 **Suggest a suitable performance measure for the quality of finished goods from a production line.**

3 A bakery will throw away bread rolls made during the day if they have not properly risen.

   What performance indicators might the production manager use to monitor this?

4 A travel firm employs five sales representatives to sell holidays.

   Suggest an appropriate performance indicator to measure productivity against budget.

5 A pizza restaurant has three ovens, each with five shelves that can fit one pizza per shelf.

   Suggest an appropriate performance indicator relating to capacity.

Chapter 1: Cost classification and behaviour

1 The correct answers are:

Overtime costs of production workers – Production department

Depreciation of cars used by sales staff – Sales department

Training course for sales director – Sales department

Advertising posters – Marketing department

2 The cost behaviour demonstrated by this cost is $\boxed{\text{Semi-variable}}$

3 The budgeted cost for supervisors is £ $\boxed{60,000}$ (as three supervisors are needed to cover 270,000 units at a cost of £20,000 each).

This cost exhibits $\boxed{\text{stepped}}$ behaviour.

4 The correct answer is: **True**.

10,000 units	Cost per unit	£43,600/10,000	=	£4.36
12,000 units	Cost per unit	£52,320/12,000	=	£4.36

As the cost per unit is the same at each level of production, this would appear to be a purely variable cost.

5 The correct answers are:

	Fixed costs (£)	Cost per unit (£ to nearest 1p)
(a) 3,000 units?	64,000	21.33
(b) 10,000 units?	64,000	6.40
(c) 16,000 units?	64,000	4.00

Workings

(a) Total fixed cost = £64,000

Fixed cost per unit £64,000/3,000 = £21.33

(b) Total fixed cost = £64,000

Fixed cost per unit £64,000/10,000 = £6.40

(c) Total fixed cost = £64,000

Fixed cost per unit £64,000/16,000 = £4.00

6   Cost of the production staff canteen → | Activity based charge to production cost centres |

Redecorating reception area → | Allocate to administrative overheads |

Machine maintenance → | Charge to production in a machine hour overhead rate |

Sick pay for production workers → | Charge to production in a labour hour overhead rate |

7   Since production is so machine-intensive, overheads should be absorbed on the basis of machine hours, so the overhead absorption rate = £180,000/30,000 = £6 per machine hour.

8

	Cutting	Finishing
Reapportioned store overheads (£)	80,000	20,000
Overhead absorption rate (see working)	£1.45 per labour hour	£3.08 per labour hour

Costs per unit	GH (£)	JK (£)
Direct materials	20.00	12.00
Direct labour (24.00 + 6.40) (16.00 + 3.20)	30.40	19.20
Overheads (4.35 + 3.08) (2.90 + 1.54)	7.43	4.44
Total cost per unit	57.83	35.64

Workings

Absorption rate

	Cutting £	Finishing £	Stores £
Allocated and apportioned overheads	225,000	180,000	100,000
Stores – re-apportioned	80,000	20,000	(100,000)
	305,000	200,000	–

Total budgeted labour hours

(3 × 50,000) + (2 × 30,000)	210,000	
(1 × 50,000) + (0.5 × 30,000)		65,000

Overhead absorption rate	£305,000	£200,000
	210,000	65,000
	£1.45 per labour hour	£3.08 per labour hour

Cost per unit			**GH**	**JK**
			£	£
Direct materials			20.00	12.00
Direct labour –	Cutting		24.00	16.00
	Finishing		6.40	3.20
Overheads –	Cutting	3 × £1.45	4.35	
		2 × £1.45		2.90
	Finishing	1 × £3.08	3.08	
		0.5 × £3.08		1.54
Total cost per unit			57.83	35.64

9   Overheads should be absorbed on an activity basis as follows:

Stores costs = £ 437.5 per materials

Production setup costs = £ 1,000 per setup

Quality control costs = £ 2,000 per inspection

The budgeted cost per unit of LM is £ 9.78

The budgeted cost per unit of NP is £ 27.41

Workings

Stores cost	=	£140,000 / 320
	=	£437.50 per materials requisition
Production setup costs	=	£280,000 / 280
	=	£1,000 per set up
Quality control costs	=	£180,000 / 90
	=	£2,000 per inspection

Product costs		LM	NP
		£	£
Direct materials	50,000 × £2.60	130,000	
	20,000 × £3.90		78,000
Direct labour	50,000 × £3.50	175,000	
	20,000 × £2.70		54,000
Stores costs	100 × £437.50	43,750	
	220 × £437.50		96,250
Production setup costs	80 × £1,000	80,000	
	200 × £1,000		200,000
Quality control costs	30 × £2,000	60,000	
	60 × £2,000		120,000
Total cost		488,750	548,250
Cost per unit		£488,750	£548,250
		50,000	20,000
		= £9.78	= £27.41

Chapter 2: Forecasting data

1

Information required	Source
Budgeted units of production per product	Production planning manager
Price of materials	Buyer
Sales brochure costs	Marketing director
Mortgage interest on factory	Finance director

2   Time series analysis using moving averages or indexing can be used.

3   The three main sources of information for sales forecasts are the sales personnel in the business, market research and time series analysis.

The key **sales personnel** of the business or the 'on-the-road salespeople' have the best first-hand knowledge of the current sales position and future potential sales. They may not necessarily be able to provide accurate forecasts of future sales but they should be able to provide an overview of the future situation and give any forecaster a feel for the future position.

Market research is expensive and probably only of particular use during the launch of a new product or the major modification of an existing product. This research will involve finding the opinions of potential consumers of the product through interviews, questionnaires or focus groups.

Time series analysis is a further way of forecasting future sales on the basis of historical sales, done by analysing past sales patterns to determine the trend of sales and any seasonal variations. The trend can then be extrapolated

into future periods and the relevant seasonal variations applied in order to determine the forecast sales for the future periods. Limitations are that a large amount of historical data is required; it assumes that the past is representative of the future and it may be hard to isolate cyclical changes due to the nature of the economy.

4 The correct answers are:

Quarter 1	163,415
Quarter 2	129,809
Quarter 3	102,477
Quarter 4	185,739

Workings

Before extrapolating the sales from the Q4 20X1 figure, we need to strip out its seasonal variation to find the underlying trend value:

$$\frac{175,000}{1.25} = 140,000$$

This trend value can now be extrapolated as a basis for the required forecasts.

Quarter 1	Trend	140,000 × 1.015	142,100
	Forecast	142,100 × 1.15	163,415
Quarter 2	Trend	142,100 × 1.015	144,232
	Forecast	144,232 × 0.90	129,809
Quarter 3	Trend	144,232 × 1.015	146,395
	Forecast	146,395 × 0.70	102,477
Quarter 4	Trend	146,395 × 1.015	148,591
	Forecast	148,591 × 1.25	185,739

5 The correct answers are:

Quarter 1	176,400
Quarter 2	159,450
Quarter 3	254,172
Quarter 4	267,156

Workings

Quarter 1	210,000 × 0.84	=	176,400
Quarter 2	212,600 × 0.75	=	159,450
Quarter 3	215,400 × 1.18	=	254,172
Quarter 4	217,200 × 1.23	=	267,156

6 Development stage
   Launch stage
   Growth stage
   Maturity stage
   Decline stage

7 A PEST analysis is based around considerations of political, economic, social and technological factors. The political factors will include any legislation such as minimum wage requirements that affect the business. The economic factors will include the current state of the economy, interest rates, inflation rates and foreign currency exchange rates, amongst others. The social factors to be considered are social aspects of life that have an impact on product output such as changes in lifestyle, fashions and tastes etc. Technological factors will include changes in technology, which affect not only the products demanded in the market, but also the production methods.

8

	Jan	Feb	Mar	Apr	May	Jun
Forecast variable production costs £	17,036	18,831	21,201	18,713	19,083	19,775
Forecast variable selling costs £	7,531	7,864	8,031	8,077	8,615	8,678

Workings

Production costs

	Jan	Feb	Mar	Apr	May	June
Production – units	1,200	1,320	1,480	1,280	1,300	1,340
Un-indexed cost £ (142.3)	16,800	18,480	20,720	17,920	18,200	18,760
Index	144.3	145.0	145.6	148.6	149.2	150.0
Indexed cost £	17,036 (W1)	18,831 (W2)	21,201 (W3)	18,713 (W4)	19,083 (W5)	19,775 (W6)

	Jan	Feb	Mar	Apr	May	June
Sales – units	1,250	1,300	1,320	1,320	1,400	1,400
Un-indexed cost £ (121.0)	7,500	7,800	7,920	7,920	8,400	8,400
Index	121.5	122.0	122.7	123.4	124.1	125.0
Indexed cost £	7,531 (W7)	7,864 (W8)	8,031 (W9)	8,077 (W10)	8,615 (W11)	8,678 (W12)

Workings

W1: $16,800 \times (144.3/142.3) = 17,036$

W2: $18,480 \times (145.0/142.3) = 18,831$

W3: $20,720 \times (145.6/142.3) = 21,201$

W4: $17,920 \times (148,6/142.3) = 18,713$

W5: $18,200 \times (149.2/142.3) = 19,083$

W6: $18,760 \times (150.0/142.3) = 19,775$

W7: $7,500 \times (121.5/121.0) = 7,531$

W8: $7,800 \times (122.0/121.0) = 7,864$

W9: $7,920 \times (122.7/121.0) = 8,031$

W10: $8,400 \times (123.4/121.0) = 8,077$

W11: $8,400 \times (124.1/121.0) = 8,615$

W12: $8,400 \times (125.0/121.0) = 8,678$

Chapter 3: Budgetary control systems

1   A budget is a formalised numerical plan for the future actions of a business. Uses of a budget are:

Planning – the setting of a budget allows management to implement strategic plans.

Control – management are also required to control the activities of the business and one method of doing this is to compare the actual result to the budgeted figures in order to report variances from budget.

Authorisation – budgets are used for authorisation of managers in terms of expenditure, and for co-ordination between the different departments and functions of an organisation.

2   In a bottom up system of budgeting, the budget holders will typically be operational managers and they will have at least some input into the setting of the budget for the resource for which they are responsible. The degree of managerial input will depend upon the policy of a particular organisation, but in a typical system, the manager may draft the initial budget. It will then be

submitted to the budget committee and will be checked to ensure that it is in harmony with other resources and production/sales budgets. There may well then be a period of negotiation between the budget holders and the budget committee until a compromise is reached between what the budget committee wants and what the manager believes is feasible.

When all of the resource budgets have been agreed, the budget officer will produce the master budget, made up of a budgeted statement of profit or loss, a budgeted statement of financial position and a cash budget.

3   The draft budget is ready for review: | The budget committee |

The managing director needs help in interpreting the draft budget:

| The budget officer |

4   Performance related pay is a system of offering managers or employees some form of bonus or other incentive if particular performance targets are met. It can be argued that performance related pay can help to ensure that there is goal congruence between the managers and the organisation; however, in order for this to happen, the system must have the following elements:

- The target that is set must be perceived by the managers as attainable, although it should also be challenging.

- The measurement of actual performance must be accurate.

- The managers must feel that they have control over all of the costs and/or revenues that are being compared to a target.

- The managers must not feel that meeting the target is dependent upon another manager's performance.

- The rewards being offered by the performance related package must be desirable enough to motivate the manager to meet the target.

If any of these elements are not in place, then the performance related pay system may serve to demotivate managers, rather than fulfilling the aim of motivating the managers to meet corporate goals.

Chapter 4: Budget preparation

1   **Units of product**

	Period 1	Period 2	Period 3
Opening inventory	1,140	1,200	1,350
Production (bal fig)	3,860	4,150	4,410
Units required	5,000	5,350	5,760
Sales	3,800	4,000	4,500
Closing inventory	1,200	1,350	1,260
Units required	5,000	5,350	5,760

Workings

Closing inventory

Period 1	4,000 units × 30%	=	1,200 units
Period 2	4,500 units × 30%	=	1,350 units
Period 3	4,200 units × 30%	=	1,260 units

2 **Units of product**

	Period 1	Period 2	Period 3
Production (from test 1)	3,860	4,150	4,410
Actual production (rounded up)	4,064	4,369	4,642

Workings

Actual production needed = production units required × 100/95

3 The correct answers are:

- The materials usage budget in units is $\boxed{53,334}$
- The materials purchasing budget in units is $\boxed{51,846}$
- The materials purchasing budget in £ is $\boxed{248,861}$

Workings

Materials usage budget – units

Production requirements

Period 1: 12,000 × 4 kg × 100/90	53,334
Period 2: 11,000 × 4 kg × 100/90	48,889

Materials purchasing budget – units

Material usage	53,334
Less opening inventory	(18,600)
Add closing inventory	
48,889 × 35%	17,112
	51,846

Materials purchasing budget – £

51,846 × £4.80	£248,861

(**Note.** Amounts are rounded up to ensure sufficient availability)

4 The correct answers are:

The production budget for the quarter is $\boxed{43,334}$ units.

The labour usage budget for the quarter is $\boxed{164,858}$ hours.

Workings

Production budget – units

Sales quantity	42,000
Less opening inventory	(7,000)
Add closing inventory	8,334
Production quantity	43,334

Labour usage budget – hours

Hours required
43,334 × 3.5 × 100/92   164,858 hours

5   The correct answers are:

Overhead cost £	Quarter 2	Quarter 3
Light and heat	76,896	85,680
Maintenance	82,090	90,325
Leasing	15,600	20,400
Rent and rates	21,000	21,000

Workings

Overhead budget – £

	Quarter 2 £	Quarter 3 £
Light and heat		
16,020 × £4.80	76,896	
17,850 × £4.80		85,680
Maintenance (W)		
(16,020 × £4.50) + £10,000	82,090	
(17,850 × £4.50) + £10,000		90,325
Leasing	15,600	20,400
Rent and rates £84,000/4	21,000	21,000

Maintenance department costs working

	Activity level	Cost
	13,000 units	£68,500
	17,000 units	£86,500
Increase	4,000 units	£18,000

Variable element	=	£18,000/4,000 units
	=	£4.50 per unit

Fixed element

	£
Variable element 13,000 units × £4.50	58,500
Fixed element (bal fig)	10,000
Total cost	68,500

6 (a) **Production budget** | 255 | **units**

Production = sales + closing inventory − opening inventory

	Units	Units
Budgeted sales		280
Opening inventory	(30)	
Closing inventory	5	
Decrease in inventory		(25)
Budgeted production		255

(b) **Materials usage budget** | 1,785 | **kg costing £** | 89,250 |

Budgeted production	255 units
× usage per unit	× 7 kg
Total budgeted usage in kg	1,785 kg
× budgeted cost per kg	× £50
Total budgeted usage in £	£89,250

(c) **Labour cost budget £** | 25,570 |

Labour cost budget – Grade O

Budgeted production	255 units
× hrs per unit	× 2 hrs
Total budgeted labour hrs	510 hrs
× budgeted cost per hr	× £15
Budgeted labour cost	£7,650

Labour cost budget – Grade R

Budgeted production	255 units
× hrs per unit	× 3 hrs
Total budgeted labour hrs	765 hrs

Note that the budgeted labour cost is not dependent on the hours worked.

Budgeted labour cost = 16 × £280 × 4 weeks = £17,920

Total labour cost budget in £ = £ (17,920 + 7,650) = £25,570

7 The correct answer is: ☐ 27,009 ☐ kg

		Kg	Kg
Material issued to production	(J: 450 × 25 kg)		11,250
	(K: 710 × 40 kg)		28,400
			39,650
Opening inventory		(40,000)	
Closing inventory		27,359	
Decrease in inventory			(12,641)
Purchases			27,009

8 **(a)** **Budgeted labour hours** ☐ 4,460 ☐

Labour hours required for production of X (W1)	2,100
Labour hours required for production of Y (W2)	2,360
Total labour hours required	4,460
Basic hours available (W3)	4,375
Overtime hours	85

Workings

W1 Labour hours required = 420 units × 5 hours per unit = 2,100 hours

W2 Labour hours required = 590 units × 4 hours per unit = 2,360 hours

W3 Basic hours available = 35 hours × 5 weeks × 25 employees = 4,375 hours

(b) **Cost of labour budget £** ☐ 44,812.50 ☐

	£
Basic wages during Period 7 (W1)	43,750.00
Overtime (W2)	1,062.50
	44,812.50

Workings

W1 Basic wages = £10 × 4,375 hours (from (a)) = £43,750

W2 Overtime = overtime hours × £ (10 × 125%) per overtime hour = 85 hours (from (a)) × £12.50 = £1,062.50

9   The correct answers are:

	Service 1	Service 2	Service 3	Service 4
Revenue budget (£)	211,680	170,100	158,760	302,400
Number of employees	7	4.5	3.5	5
Direct wages budget (£)	94,080	75,600	64,680	117,600

Workings

(a)   Revenue budget

Service

1   £20 × 10,584 = £211,680
2   £25 × 6,804 = £170,100
3   £30 × 5,292 = £158,760
4   £40 × 7,560 = £302,400

(b)   No of employees required/department =

$$\frac{\text{Budgeted chargeable hours}}{35 \times 48} \times 100/90$$

Service

1   (10,584 × 100/90)/(35 × 48) = 7.0
2   (6,804 × 100/90)/(35 × 48) = 4.5
3   (5,292 × 100/90)/(35 × 48) = 3.5
4   (7,560 × 100/90)/(35 × 48) = 5.0

The business should employ the following staff:

Service	Number of full time	Number of part time
1	7	0
2	4	1
3	3	1
4	5	0
Total	19	2

(c) Direct wages budget

Service		£
1	£8 an hour × 7.0 employees × 35 hours a week × 48 weeks	94,080
2	£10 an hour × 4.5 employees × 35 hours a week × 48 weeks	75,600
3	£11 an hour × 3.5 employees × 35 hours a week × 48 weeks	64,680
4	£14 an hour × 5.0 employees × 35 hours a week × 48 weeks	117,600

Chapter 5: Preparing cash budgets

1   **Forecast cash receipts**

	January	February	March
Budgeted cash receipts from sales (£)	695,500	677,000	683,000

Workings

		January £	February £	March £
Cash sales (10% of sales figure)		70,000	73,000	76,000
Credit sales	40% × 720,000	288,000		
	40% × 700,000		280,000	
	40% × 730,000			292,000
	45% × 750,000	337,500		
	45% × 720,000		324,000	
	45% × 700,000			315,000
		695,500	677,000	683,000

2   **Forecast cash payments**

	January	February	March
Budgeted cash payments for purchases (£)	560,340	538,275	529,560

Workings

Purchases

	October £	November £	December £	January £	February £
75% of sales	592,500	562,500	540,000	525,000	547,500

Cash payments

	January £	February £	March £
October purchases			
592,500 × 15%	88,875		
November purchases			
562,500 × 65%	365,625		
562,500 × 15%		84,375	
December purchases			
540,000 × 20% × 98%	105,840		
540,000 × 65%		351,000	
540,000 × 15%			81,000
January purchases			
525,000 × 20% × 98%		102,900	

	January £	February £	March £
525,000 × 65%			341,250
February purchases			
547,500 × 20% × 98%			107,310
	560,340	538,275	529,560

3 Cash budget for the quarter ending 31 December

	October £	November £	December £
Cash receipts:			
Sales proceeds from equipment	0	4,000	0
Cash payments:			
Wages	42,000	42,000	42,000
General overheads (W1)	25,000	29,800	31,000
New equipment	0	40,000	0

Workings

Working 1 – General overheads

	October £	November £	December £
September overheads			
(30,000 – 5,000) × 20%	5,000		
October overheads			
(30,000 – 5,000) × 80%	20,000		
(30,000 – 5,000) × 20%		5,000	
November overheads			
(36,000 – 5,000) × 80%		24,800	
(36,000 – 5,000) × 20%			6,200
December overheads			
(36,000 – 5,000) × 80%			24,800
	25,000	29,800	31,000

4 The correct answer is: £270,000.

Proceeds = carrying amount + profits = £212,000 + £58,000 = £270,000.

Chapter 6: Budget preparation – limiting factors

1

	Jan	Feb	Mar	Apr	May	June	Total
Materials required – kg	2,600	3,100	3,000	3,100	2,800	3,200	17,800
Material purchases	3,000	3,000	3,000	3,000	3,000	3,000	18,000
Excess/(shortage)	400	(100)	–	(100)	200	(200)	(200)

There is an overall excess in availability over requirements of 200 kg if 3,000 kg are purchased each month. To minimise inventory levels, the shortages in February and April can be made up for by buying only 200 kg more than is needed in January, so 2,800 kg should be bought in January. In every other month, 3,000 kg should be bought. The shortage of 200 kg in June is made up for by buying in May 200 kg more than is required for production in that month.

2   This appears to be a long-term labour shortage, so the business should have two aims:

(a)   To increase the availability of the required level of labour as soon as possible.

(b)   To attempt to lessen the problem in the short term before the additional labour becomes available.

The longer-term options in order to acquire more highly skilled labour are:

- To recruit additional highly skilled staff
- To train existing staff to this skill level

In the shorter term, until the recruitment or training reaps rewards, the options are:

- To increase the overtime worked by the existing employees
- To use agency workers
- To sub-contract the work
- To use finished goods inventory to satisfy sales demand
- To buy in the finished goods

3   As this is a short-term issue, the business could try the following:

- Use of material held in inventory – these could be run down in order to maintain production and sales.

- Use of finished goods held in inventory – in order to maintain sales in the short term, finished goods inventory can be run down, even though production levels are not as high as would be liked.

- Rescheduling purchases – if the amount of the material required is available in some periods but not in others, then the materials purchases could be rescheduled to ensure that the maximum use is made of the available materials.

4 The limiting factor is $\boxed{\text{labour hours}}$

Workings

Material required for sales demand = 15,000 × 0.5 = 7,500 kg
Material available = 9,000 kg, so not a limiting factor
Labour required for sales demand = 15,000 × (24/60) = 6,000 hours
Labour hours available = 30 × 180 = 5,400 hours

Therefore, labour is the limiting factor, unless overtime can be paid.

5 The correct answer is:

Product	Manufactured to maximise profit
Product A	
Product B	✓

Workings

Per unit	Product A	Product B
Sales price £	13	8
Direct materials £ 2 × 2 1.5 × 2	(4)	(3)
Direct labour £ 0.5 × 10 0.25 × 10	(5)	(2.5)
Variable overhead £	(1)	(0.5)
Contribution £	3	2
Contribution per labour hour (£3/0.5) (£2/0.25)	6	8

Product B gives the greater contribution per labour hour and so should be the one produced.

Chapter 7: Budgetary control – comparing budget and actual costs

1   A fixed budget is prepared in advance of the budget period and serves as an overall plan of what the business is aiming for during the budget period. It ensures that all areas of the business are co-ordinated in their activities.

A flexed budget is prepared at the end of the budget period and is based upon the actual activity level during the period. It shows the standard cost of the actual production for the month and is used for control purposes, as the actual costs are compared to these standard costs to produce variances.

2   The correct answer is:

Original budget		Flexed budget	Actual	Variance	Fav/Adv
4,000	Sales volume (units)	3,600	3,600		
£		£	£	£	
96,000	Sales revenue 3,600 × £24	86,400	90,000	3,600	Fav
18,000	Materials 3,600 × £4.50	16,200	15,120	1,080	Fav
27,200	Labour 3,600 × £6.80	24,480	25,200	720	Adv
5,700	Production overhead	5,700	5,900	200	Adv
45,100	Gross profit	40,020	43,780	3,760	Fav
35,200	General expenses (W)	32,800	32,880	80	Adv
9,900	Operating profit	7,220	10,900	3,680	Fav

Working – General expenses

Variable element of cost	=	£35,200 – £11,200
	=	£24,000
Variable cost per unit	=	£24,000/4,000
	=	£6 per unit
Cost at 3,600 units	=	3,600 × £6 + £11,200
	=	£32,800

3 Operating statement: January

	Flexed budget 30,000 units		Actual 30,000 units		Variance
	£	£	£	£	£
Sales revenue		90,000		86,000	4,000 Adv
Materials	24,000		22,500		1,500 Fav
Labour	39,000		41,200		2,200 Adv
Production expenses	5,600		5,800		200 Adv
Production cost		68,600		69,500	900 Adv
Gross profit		21,400		16,500	4,900 Adv
General expenses		15,000		14,700	300 Fav
Operating profit		6,400		1,800	4,600 Adv

Workings

Sales

24,000 – standard selling price per unit	=	£72,000/24,000	
	=	£3 per unit	

28,000 – standard selling price per unit	=	£84,000/28,000	
	=	£3 per unit	

The sales revenue is thus strictly variable.

30,000 – standard sales income	=	30,000 × £3	
	=	£90,000	

Materials

24,000 – standard cost per unit	=	£19,200/24,000	
	=	£0.80	

28,000 – standard cost per unit	=	£22,400/28,000	
	=	£0.80	

The materials cost is thus strictly variable.

30,000 – standard materials cost	=	30,000 × £0.80	
	=	£24,000	

Labour

24,000 – standard cost per unit	=	£33,000/24,000
	=	£1.375

28,000 – standard cost per unit	=	£37,000/28,000
	=	£1.32

We may assume, then, that labour is a semi-variable cost.

Semi-variable labour cost

Increase in cost per unit increase	=	£4,000/4,000 units
	=	£1 per unit
Fixed element	=	£33,000 – (24,000 × £1)
	=	£9,000
30,000 – standard labour cost	=	(£1 × 30,000) + £9,000
	=	£39,000

Production expenses – fixed cost

General expenses

24,000 – cost per unit	=	£12,600/24,000
	=	£0.525

28,000 – cost per unit	=	£14,200/28,000
	=	£0.507

We may assume, then, that general expenses are a semi-variable cost.

Semi-variable general expense cost

Increase in cost per unit increase	=	£1,600/4,000 units
	=	£0.40 per unit

Fixed element	=	£12,600 – (24,000 × £0.40)
	=	£3,000

30,000 – labour cost	=	(£0.40 × 30,000) + £3,000
	=	£15,000

4 Marginal costing budget

	£	£
Sales revenue		900,000
Materials	216,000	
Labour	324,000	
Cost of production (54,000 units)	540,000	
Less: closing inventory (4,000 units)	(40,000)	
Cost of sales		(500,000)
Gross profit		400,000
Fixed production overhead		(108,000)
Fixed general expenses		(198,000)
Net profit		94,000

Absorption costing profit   =   £102,000
Marginal costing profit   =   £94,000

The difference of £8,000 is due to the difference in closing inventory valuation: £48,000 under absorption costing and £40,000 under marginal costing. This represents the share of fixed overheads carried forward in inventory under absorption costing: $\left(4000 \times \dfrac{108,000}{54,000} \right)$

5 Budgeted fixed overheads = £1.90 × 240,000 = £456,000

Variance = £480,000 − £456,000 = $\boxed{£24,000}$ $\boxed{\text{Adverse}}$.

6

A controllable cost is one over which the manager of a responsibility centre has influence. If a manager's performance is to be judged, then it must only be judged on the basis of costs or revenues over which the manager has control. If uncontrollable costs are included then this could have a demotivating effect on the manager.

7 REPORT

To: Management Team
From: Management Accountant
Date: xx.xx.xx
Subject: **Format of variance report**

Following my meeting with the product manager last week, I have undertaken a review of the format of the variance report used throughout the organisation. I have concluded that, because of the way in which the information is presented, the report could be potentially misleading for users. I therefore recommend that the format be adapted as follows.

- Information about volumes (hours, kg and so on) should be reported separately in order to make the report less confusing and easier to read and understand. All information on the monthly variance report, except that concerning production volumes, should be monetary.

- The volume variances (those in hours, kg and so on) should be converted into monetary amounts in order for the financial implications of the variances to become more obvious.

- Instead of calculating variances by comparing actual results and the original fixed budget results, actual results should be compared with budget results, flexed to the actual production volumes. The flexed results provide a far more realistic and fair target against which to measure actual results. For example, the direct labour (£) variance is currently calculated by comparing the budgeted labour cost of producing 10,000 units with the actual labour cost of producing 9,905 units. A revised format should show a direct labour (£) variance calculated by comparing the actual direct labour cost with the budgeted direct labour cost of producing 9,905 units.

- The report shows no flexed budget figures (the results which would have been expected at the actual production level achieved). A flexed budget column should therefore be included in the report.

- The report does not provide a narrative description of any known reasons for the variances. Explanations would increase the report's user-friendliness.

- The report should use the principles of exception reporting, highlighting the most important variances in order to direct management attention to areas where action is most urgently required.

- Controllable fixed costs (If they exist) should be included on the report and separately identified.

A recommended layout for the monthly variance report is shown in the Appendix to this report. An identical format could be used for the presentation of cumulative results to date.

Appendix

Monthly variance report

	Original fixed budget Units	Flexed budget Units	Actual results Units	Total variance £	Total variance %	Notes
Production volume	X	X	X			
Variable costs						
Direct material	X	X	X	X	X	
Direct labour	X	X	X	X	X	
Total variable costs	X	X	X	X	X	
Controllable fixed costs	X	X	X	X	X	
Total costs	X	X	X	X	X	

The notes column could be used to provide an explanation of the reasons for various variances occurring and/or to highlight important variances.

Chapter 8: Performance indicators in budgetary control

1 Productivity measures include:

- Number of customers served per hour/day

- Number of customers served per cashier in a shift

- Value of goods processed through till per cashier or per hour

- Number of customers per queue at different times of day/different cashiers

Other performance measures may include:

- Number of calls made to supervisor per shift/per cashier
- Number of customer complaints (if any) per cashier
- Time spent per cashier serving no customers (idle time)
- Cost of idle time as a percentage of cashier labour costs

Tutorial note. Remember to include simple, visual measures such as the number of customers in the queue. These are not just a factor of the productivity of the cashiers but the demand of customers at particular times, but by knowing this, the manager can plan accordingly.

2 Number of defective units

Cost of defective units

Percentage of production which is defective

Tutorial note. Only one of these measures was required

3 Number of bread rolls thrown away per day/shift

Cost of bread rolls thrown away (ingredients, labour, machine costs of baking)

Percentage of bread rolls produced which are defective

4 Productivity could be measured in terms of the number of holidays sold per sales representative, or the number of holidays sold per day.

5 Number of ovens/shelves in use during a shift

Percentage of ovens/shelves in use during a shift

Synoptic assessment preparation

Questions

1

(a) **Which ONE of the following statements correctly describes the contents of the statement of financial position?**

    A   A list of ledger balances shown in debit and credit columns

    B   A list of all the assets owned and all the liabilities owed by a business

    C   A record of income generated and expenditure incurred over a given period

    D   A record of the amount of cash generated and used by a company in a given period.

(b) A supplier sends you a statement showing a balance outstanding of £14,350. Your own records show a balance outstanding of £14,500.

Which one of the following could be the reason for this difference?

    A   The supplier sent an invoice for £150 which you have not yet received.

    B   The supplier has allowed you £150 cash discount which you had omitted to enter in your ledgers.

    C   You have paid the supplier £150 which he has not yet accounted for.

    D   You have returned goods worth £150 which the supplier has not yet accounted for.

2

Operational review

Review the operating statement and the additional information below, and prepare a report by email.

Operating Statement	Flexed Budget	Actual	Variance Fav/(Adv)
Sales volume		608,000 units	
	£000	£000	£000
Sales revenue	486	517	31
Variable costs			
Material	122	128	(6)
Labour	67	76	(9)

Operating Statement	Flexed Budget	Actual	Variance Fav/(Adv)
Distribution	24	21	3
Power	43	49	(6)
Equipment hire	97	0	97
Total	**353**	**274**	**79**
Contribution	**133**	**243**	**110**
Fixed costs			
Power	4	3	1
Depreciation	63	185	(122)
Marketing	11	15	(4)
Administration	14	15	(1)
Total	**92**	**218**	**(126)**
Operating profit	**41**	**25**	**(16)**

Additional information

- The budget has been flexed to the actual number of units produced and sold. The original budget was based on an expected sales volume of 750,000 units which was expected to generate a profit of £72,000.

- The original budget included £63,000 for depreciation of production machinery and £120,000 for the hire of additional machines to meet the budgeted workload. The plant engineer is responsible for both of these budgets. After the original budget was approved, he decided to purchase the additional production equipment rather than hire it. The depreciation cost was roughly the same as had been budgeted for equipment and so the standard cost of the product did not change.

- Early in the financial year, the marketing manager increased the selling price of the product. He realised that this would reduce sales volume but estimated that profit would increase.

- The chief executive cannot understand how these important strategic decisions were made without his knowledge. He also wants to know why the standard cost of the product did not increase if depreciation was more expensive than equipment hire.

Write an email to the chief executive, in three sections, in which you explain:

(1) (i) The main reasons for the sales revenue, equipment hire and depreciation variances from the flexed budget.

(ii) How the equipment hire and depreciation variances might have been avoided.

(2) How failings in the budgetary control system resulted in lower profits.

(3) Why the standard cost of the product did not increase when equipment was purchased rather than hired.

To: The Chief Executive   **From:** Budget Accountant

Subject: Review of Operating Statement   **Date:** xx xx xx

(1) Reasons for variances

(2) Budgetary control system failure

(3) **Standard cost**

Budget Accountant

3

Performance indicators

Grippit manufactures domestic wind turbines. A colleague has prepared forecast information based upon two scenarios. The forecast profit or loss account and statement of financial position for both scenarios are shown below.

- Scenario 1 is to set the price at £1,250 per unit, with sales of 10,000 units per year.

- Scenario 2 is to set the price at £1,000 per unit, with sales of 14,000 units per year.

Forecast profit or loss account

	Scenario 2 £000	Scenario 2 £000
Revenue	12,500	14,000
Cost of production:		
Direct (raw) materials	3,000	4,200
Direct labour	2,000	2,800
Fixed production overheads	3,000	3,000
Total cost of sales	8,000	10,000
Gross profit	4,500	4,000
Selling and distribution costs	1,000	1,000

	Scenario 2 £000	Scenario 2 £000
Administration costs	750	750
Operating profit	2,750	2,250
Interest payable	600	600
Net profit	2,150	1,650

Extracts from the forecast statement of financial position

	£000	£000
Non-current assets	20,000	20,000
Current assets	5,000	5,500
Current liabilities	4,600	5,800
Long-term borrowing	12,000	11,300
Net assets	8,400	8,400
Represented by:		
Share capital	5,650	6,150
Profit or loss account	2,750	2,250
Net assets	8,400	8,400

(a) Calculate the following performance indicators for each scenario:

  (i)   Gross profit margin
  (ii)   Net profit margin
  (iii)   Direct materials cost per unit
  (iv)   Direct labour cost per unit
  (v)   Fixed production cost per unit
  (vi)   Gearing ratio
  (vii) Interest cover

(b) Draft an email for the finance director covering the following:

  (i)   An explanation of why the gross profit margin is different in each scenario. Your answer should refer to the following:

  •   Sales price per unit
  •   Materials, labour and fixed cost per unit

  (ii)   An assessment of the level of gearing and interest cover and whether it is a problem for the business

(a)

		Scenario 1	Scenario 2
(i)	Gross profit margin		
(ii)	Net profit margin		
(iii)	Direct materials cost per unit		
(iv)	Direct labour cost per unit		
(v)	Fixed production cost per unit		
(vi)	Gearing ratio		
(vii)	Interest cover		

(b)

Email		
To:		Date:
From:		Subject:

(i) Why are the gross profit margins different?

- Sales price per unit

- Materials

- Labour

- Fixed costs

(ii) Assessment of level of gearing and interest cover

Answers

1

(a) B.   The statement of financial position contains a list of all the assets owned and all the liabilities owed by a business.

(b) B.   A, C and D would make the supplier's statement £150 **higher**.

2

To: The Chief Executive   **Date:**   xx xx xx

From: Budget Accountant   **Subject:**   Review of Operating Statement

(1) **Reasons for variances**

I have reviewed the results for the period. There was an operating profit of £25,000 compared with the flexed budget profit of £41,000. The original budget anticipated a profit of £72,000 based on sales of 750,000 units.

The favourable sales revenue variance over the flexed budget of £31k (6.4%) was due to an unbudgeted price increase. A consequent reduction in sales volume was expected. It is worth noting that if costs had been kept to budget at this volume (the flexed budget shows £445,000 of variable and fixed costs) the profit would have been £72,000, exactly as originally budgeted.

However, expenditure exceeded the flexed budget. The plant engineer decided to purchase production equipment rather than hire. This gave a 100% saving in hire charges. The adverse variance on depreciation was £122k. At the originally budgeted production level, the net variance would have been negligible. With a reduced volume, it would have been possible to reduce the amount of equipment hired, but the depreciation charge is fixed.

The variances on equipment hire and depreciation could have been avoided if the plant engineer had been aware of the expected volume reduction. Possibly he would have purchased less equipment, or he might have decided against any purchase and continued hiring.

(2) **Budgetary control system failure**

One of the uses of budgetary control is to create a mechanism for authorising management decisions and we seem to have overlooked this. Significant departures from the approved budget, such as the price reduction and the purchase of production equipment, need to be carefully considered, communicated and authorised.

BPP
LEARNING MEDIA

> Neither the marketing manager nor the plant engineer informed their colleagues about their plans. You, as chief executive did not authorise them. Whilst both decisions seemed reasonable in isolation, the combined effect (reducing volume at the same time as replacing variable cost with fixed) hit profits.
>
> This outcome would have been apparent if the budget had been revised to incorporate the new strategies. Furthermore, it is disconcerting that the deterioration was not identified through regular management meetings.

(3) **Standard cost**

> Standard costing is an excellent system for controlling variable costs but not so useful for fixed overheads such as depreciation.
>
> It is not surprising that the standard cost did not change when the plant engineer decided to purchase equipment if he was not aware that volume would reduce. At the original budget volume, £120,000 of equipment hire would have been replaced by a similar amount of depreciation. The unit cost would be the same.
>
> In time, the reduced volume would generate an under recovery of overheads but, as the budget had not been revised, it would not be easy to see what was going wrong.

Budget Accountant

3

(a)

		Scenario 1	Scenario 2
(i)	Gross profit margin		
	= Gross Profit/Turnover × 100	(4,500 / 12,500) × 100 = 36.00%	(4,000 / 14,000) × 100 = 28.57%
(ii)	Net profit margin		
	= Net Profit/Turnover × 100	(2,150 / 12,500) × 100 = 17.20%	(1,650 / 14,000) × 100 = 11.79%
(iii)	Direct materials cost per unit		
	= Direct materials cost/sales units	£3,000,000 / 10,000 = £300	£4,200,000 / 14,000 = £300

	Scenario 1	Scenario 2
(iv) Direct labour cost per unit		
= Direct labour cost/sales unit	£2,000,000 / 10,000 = £200	£2,8000,000 / 14,000 = £200
(v) Fixed production cost per unit		
= Fixed production cost/sales units	£3,000,000 / 10,000 = £300	£3,000,000 / 14,000 = £214.29
(vi) Gearing ratio		
= Debt/(debt + equity)	12,000 / (12,000 + 8,400) =	11,300 / (11,300 + 8,400) =
	(0.5881 or 58.82%)	0.5736 or 57.36%
Alternative answer for gearing:		
Gearing ratio		
= Debt/equity	12,000 / 8,400 =	11,300 / 8,400 =
	(1.4286 or 142.86%)	(1.3452 or 134.52%)
(vii) Interest cover		
= Operating profit/interest payable	2,750 / 600 = 4.58	2.250/600 = 3.75

(b)

Email

To: Finance Director

From: AAT Trainee

Date: 16 June 20X8

Subject: Gross profit margin, gearing and interest cover

(i) Gross profit margin

The gross profit margin for scenario 1 is 36% and scenario 2 is 28.57%. Direct materials and labour are the same under both scenarios so that the higher gross profit margin for scenario 1 must be as result of differences in sales price per unit or fixed production overheads. In fact, the fixed costs per unit are higher under scenario 1 because less volume is produced (£300 per unit as opposed to £213.29 per unit for scenario 2). Therefore, the reason for the higher gross margin is the higher price unit (£1,250 and £1,000 respectively).

(ii) Gearing and interest cover

The level of gearing for both scenarios is at a similar level. Everything else being equal, the higher the gearing ratio, the higher the risk. This is because debt has interest payments that have to be made from operating profit. However, the gearing indicator cannot be considered in isolation.

The level of interest cover shows how many times Grippit can pay its interest payable out of operating profit. For scenario 1, the profit is 4.58 times greater than interest payable. This falls slightly to 3.75 times for scenario 2 due to the fall in profits, as the interest payable is constant under both scenarios.

Both scenarios have a relatively high interest cover and this does not appear to be a problem for the business.

Bibliography

Brown, J L. and Howard, L.R. (2002). Principles and Practice of Management Accountancy. London, Macdonald & Evans Ltd.

Vernon, Raymond. (1966) International Investment and International Trade in the Product Cycle. The Quarterly Journal of Economics. [Online] 80 (2), 190-207. Available from: http://www.jstor.org/stable/1880689 [Accessed 25 May 2016].

Index

W

Wastage of materials, 218

Z

Zero based budgeting (ZBB), 91

REVIEW FORM

How have you used this Course Book?
(Tick one box only)

☐ Self study

☐ On a course_____

☐ Other _____

Why did you decide to purchase this Course Book? *(Tick one box only)*

☐ Have used BPP materials in the past

☐ Recommendation by friend/colleague

☐ Recommendation by a college lecturer

☐ Saw advertising

☐ Other _____

During the past six months do you recall seeing/receiving either of the following?
(Tick as many boxes as are relevant)

☐ Our advertisement in Accounting Technician

☐ Our Publishing Catalogue

Which (if any) aspects of our advertising do you think are useful?
(Tick as many boxes as are relevant)

☐ Prices and publication dates of new editions

☐ Information on Course Book content

☐ Details of our free online offering

☐ None of the above

Your ratings, comments and suggestions would be appreciated on the following areas of this Course Book.

	Very useful	Useful	Not useful
Chapter overviews	☐	☐	☐
Introductory section	☐	☐	☐
Quality of explanations	☐	☐	☐
Illustrations	☐	☐	☐
Chapter activities	☐	☐	☐
Test your learning	☐	☐	☐
Keywords	☐	☐	☐

	Excellent	Good	Adequate	Poor
Overall opinion of this Course Book	☐	☐	☐	☐

Do you intend to continue using BPP Products?   ☐ Yes ☐ No

Please note any further comments and suggestions/errors on the reverse of this page and return it to: Nisar Ahmed, AAT Head of Programme, BPP Learning Media Ltd, FREEPOST, London, W12 8AA.

Alternatively, the Head of Programme of this edition can be emailed at: nisarahmed@bpp.com.

REVIEW FORM (continued)

TELL US WHAT YOU THINK

Please note any further comments and suggestions/errors below